Information Technology
and Management Control

INFORMATION TECHNOLOGY AND MANAGEMENT CONTROL

An Agency Theory Perspective

ZEINAB A. KARAKE

Westport, Connecticut
London

Library of Congress Cataloging-in-Publication Data

Karake, Zeinab A.
    Information technology and management control : an agency theory
perspective / Zeinab A. Karake.
        p.   cm.
    Includes bibliographical references and index.
    ISBN 0-275-94198-1 (alk. paper)
    1. Management information systems.   2. Information technology.
I. Title.
    T58.6.K367   1992
    658.4'038—dc20   91-44007

British Library Cataloguing in Publication Data is available.

Library of Congress Catalog Card Number: 91-44007
ISBN: 0-275-94198-1

First published in 1992

Praeger Publishers, 88 Post Road West, Westport, CT 06881
An imprint of Greenwood Publishing Group, Inc.

Printed in the United States of America

∞™

The paper used in this book complies with the
Permanent Paper Standard issued by the National
Information Standards Organization (Z39.48-1984).

10 9 8 7 6 5 4 3 2 1

To my guiding light, my husband Victor,
and the joy of my life, my daughter Rana.

Contents

Information Technology
and Management Control

1

Establishing the Context

The recent explosion of information and information technology (IT) has induced corporate management to utilize its ingenuity in creating the best available means to manage the flow of information, control flow channels, and integrate the different assets (both hardware and software) of information technology utilized by the different departments and divisions of the corporation. As companies invest heavily in information-based systems, they are vesting more control in technology strategists and chief information officers (CIOs).

Information technology is one of the major powers affecting the direction organizations are taking in our day, and numerous terms have been used to symbolize the change that has occurred in today's society. John Naisbitt refers to this phenomenon as the global "information revolution" (Naisbitt 1982); Christopher Evans employs a more precise term when he speaks of the "computer revolution" (Evans 1980); and Alvin Toffler persuasively articulates his views of the "Third Wave" with its accompanying "intelligent environment" (Toffler 1980). Regardless of the terms chosen, the fact remains that society has undergone a major transformation. No longer based on industry, today's society is one based on information.

The reality of the information age is well documented, and the work force statistics support its existence. Compared to the 1950s, when no more than 17 percent of the work force was engaged in information-related jobs, more than 65 percent of today's work force is categorized as information/knowledge workers. Morton F. Meltzer describes the influence of computers in creating the information age by arguing that three-fourths of all the world's information has been developed within the last 20 years (Meltzer 1981: 17).

The information age has forced U.S. businesses to change their perceptions of information, information systems, and information technology. Various terms have been used to mean information, each one signifying the importance that business now places on it. Robert Orsey refers to information as an "asset" (Orsey 1982), while Robert Landau calls it a "resource" (Landau 1980).

Although the role of information is perceived differently by different scholars, the fact that it constitutes an integral component of global business is no longer disputable. According to Peter Drucker, "information is the manager's main tool, indeed the manager's capital" (Drucker 1980:). John Rockart of MIT's Sloan School of Management maintains that information is an "ingredient" vital to good management. Meltzer views information as having "inestimable value" and further writes, "corporations need information to compete, grow, profit, and *survive* [author's italics]...The manager who fails to focus on the information needs of his company will soon be bypassed by a new breed of managers who realize that information is the lifeblood of the corporate body" (Meltzer 1981: 65).

To help organizations solve critical business problems and provide new services by the means of collecting data, turning data into information, and turning information into knowledge quickly enough to reflect its value, organizations are investing more and more in IT. In a recent article Max Hopper, senior vice-president for information systems at American Airlines, argues that for the past 30 years, much of companies' money and energy has focused on building hardware, software, and networks powerful enough to generate useful data. According to Hopper, that challenge is close to being solved and "we have gotten our hands around the data gathering conundrum" (Hopper 1990). The next phase for competitive differentiation revolves around the intensification of analysis; as a matter of fact, "astute managers will shift their attention from systems to information," and *ultimately knowledge.* (Hopper 1990).

Many American companies have adopted various approaches to information and information technology. These approaches are based on using information strategically, creating competitive opportunities, increasing the use of technology more effectively, and enhancing more enduring connection between IT investments and strategic goals. Many businesses have accepted the notion that IT can play a strategic role by creating competitive advantage rather than simply displacing cost. Success stories in this category include American Hospital

Supply Corporation, American Airlines, Mrs. Fields Cookies, United Service Automobile Association, The Limited, and many others. To gain that competitive edge, these corporations have been using information technology in a variety of ways, like the creation of interorganizational systems that connect customers, suppliers, and competitors to the organization's computers, and origination of systems supporting strategic decisions, such as marketing analyses, cost management, control, and so on. However, numerous other companies have realized that they seldom know how to translate their wishes into specific IT investments. To be able to address the needs to build a competitive advantage, a company requires a strategy that addresses the what, why, how, and when of acquiring and using technical resources. To be effective, the IT strategy must be an integral component of the company's overall strategy, and must support the company's objectives and goals.

Managers in our day are utilizing information technology as a core element in aggressive new approaches to the marketplace or to enhance control of internal operations. Those managers have, explicitly or implicitly, realized that, in the past few years, information technology has gone through a radical change. In reality, both the applications and the effective management of information technology look very different from what they did just a few years ago. Volatility in the business environment, coupled with technology's ability to provide management with efficient communication and information is radically moving corporate management to realize that the "proactive" management of information and information technology is as critical as the management of other resources, if not more so. As a result, managers can no longer easily avoid the process of making decisions about information technology. IT affects the entire organization from its design and structure to product market strategies. Consequently, an increasing number of corporate leaders are buying into the idea that information and information technology are critical to the survival and success of their companies as the new decade emerges. Corporate leaders have realized that information and information technology are value-adding ideas and not cost-containment ones (Alter 1989), and that information technology is playing a major role in achieving productivity and quality.

As the new decade continues, the information and the speed with which corporate executives receive it will be extremely important to charting the course of any company. John Donovan, professor at MIT and chair of the Cambridge Technology Group, maintains that information executives are the only people who can improve the competitive position of U.S. corporations during the 1990s (Donovan 1989).

From the literature review on information and information technology, two fundamental observations were made. First, U.S. companies and their managers have adopted different approaches to managing IT resources. Some companies regard IT resources as being as vital as financial and human resources, and believe they should, therefore, have top management presence. Those companies have created a top management position, the chief information officer whose duty is to manage IT at the corporate level and to participate, with other management officers, in drawing the strategic paths of the corporation. The CIO in most instance reports directly to the chief executive officer (CEO) or the chief financial officer (CFO). Second, it was revealed from the preliminary review of the literature that some companies spend relatively more on IT resources than others in order to increase their performances. In some instances, these expenditures are proportional to the company's size; in other instance, they are not. This leads one to believe that other factors, in addition to size, are determinants of IT investments.

The main objective of this book is to determine those company-specific characteristics that act as determinants of (1) the creation of a top management level CIO position, and (2) the level of investment in and performance of IT.

PARADIGMS OF INFORMATION TECHNOLOGY

Many essays concerning the implications of information technology assert that these implications take a particular form and that the broad outlines of the future with IT can be discerned fairly rapidly. The review of the literature on this issue uncovered an array of different conclusions. According to the various authors, the implications could be either centralizing or decentralizing, either deskilling or upgrading, either enhancing or threatening democracy, and so on, through a list of oppositions (See Miles 1989: 222). The literature revealed three distinct perspectives on the implications of IT. The three such viewpoints are labeled the *continuity, transformation,* and *structural* schools.

For continuists, IT exemplifies an incremental step on a long course of technological development. The important determinant for IT innovation here is how technological changes can meet (1) users' needs, (2) the structure of factor costs, and (3) the availability of managerial, technical, and work force skills (Miles 1989: 224). Corporations that do not jump on the wagon of IT innovativeness will risk the problem of loosing their competitive edge. This is the main reason why companies spend respectable percentages of their budgets on technological research and development (R&D).

Transformationists tend to put less importance on structures and strategies than on their underlying values and perspectives (Miles 1989). Consequently, there has been ample research into perceptions of the "impact" of IT on the work place. Following the 1982 Versailles Summit, a major program of research into the acceptance of new technologies was launched. The latter was particularly inspired by concerns that public resistance to change was the root of slow innovation (Miles 1989: 225).

A major assumption of the structuralists is that many of our current uncertainties relate to being at the point of transition between structural doctrines; the stagnation and limits of old structures could be clearly seen, but the viabilities of new models are hard to assess. New technologies imply learning processes and organizational changes to capitalize on their potential; new areas of demand are needed to establish new patterns of growth. Structuralist analysis typically attempts to identify key features of an emerging paradigm and to outline the enabling constraining factors around appropriate changes.

These three schools of thought differ in assessing the implications of IT on formal work (including different economic sectors), social structure, international interdependence, and globalization. It would be inappropriate to draw many conclusions from existing research, however. What is apparent is that there has been uneven development of research, and that this adds to the intrinsic difficulties associated with assessing the implications of information technology and an information society.

Most practitioners and theorists are in agreement that the majority of organizations in the 1990s will continue moving from the industrial society to the information era or the third wave. According to Huber (1984), post industrial organizations will be characterized by more and increasing knowledge, more and increasing complexity, and more and increasing turbulence. He advocates the use of information technology as an effective way of coping with the changing environment. Huber and McDaniel (1986) go one step further by arguing that the existing organizational design paradigm is declining in scope, and that the switch to a decision-making paradigm in which IT plays a critical role is essential for organizations to survive in a hostile, complex, and turbulent environment.

INFORMATION TECHNOLOGY: BENEFITS VERSUS VALUE

As a by-product of technology, information is an overriding consideration for managers. Through the years, managers have generally been preoccupied with specific types of information rather than focusing more broadly on information itself. An unfortunate consequence of this tendency has been the haphazard, bits-and-pieces management of information. Costly inefficiencies resulting from the collection of irrelevant or redundant information have too often been the result. Information management specialists have responded to this state of affairs by recommending that information be viewed as a resource.

A variety of benefits are provided by information technologies: better profits; improved communications; an evolving understanding of information requirements; a test-bed for system evolution; and cost reductions (Houdeshel & Watson 1987). The information provided by new advanced technology has characteristics that are important to management. It supports decision making by identifying areas that require attention, providing answers to questions, and giving knowledge about related areas. It provides relevant, timely information. In addition, information technology has improved communications in several ways. It is used to facilitate the sharing of information with customers and suppliers.

Before we move further, it is important to differentiate between the benefits of information and information technology and the value of these assets. Benefits of IT are evaluated by using a number of economic analysis techniques, such as return on investment, net present value, and the payback period. These techniques are based on assessing monetary costs and benefits of the various investments in IT, and conducting a structured benefit/cost analysis. Value of investment in information technology, on the other hand, goes beyond measurable benefits to include a number of intangible factors and impacts. One important factor is the strategic match of a specific investment whereby the degree to that a proposed investment responds to established business strategies and goals is assessed. Competitive advantage is another intangible factor which is hard to quantify. Evaluating the competitive advantage of an investment calls for an assessment of the degree to which the proposed investment provides an advantage in the marketplace. The management of information is another intangible factor. This is an assessment of an investment contribution to management's need for information on essential activities. Finally, competitive response is an important intangible element. This evaluates the degree of business risk associated with not undertaking the investment (Parker, Trainor & Benson 1989).

In general, to evaluate an IT investment, it is necessary to consider both tangible and intangible factors. The emphasis should be on the value of this IT investment and not solely on its benefits.

MANAGING INFORMATION TECHNOLOGY

Because the strategic information technology function has been evolving rapidly, it has affected its own structure and position within the corporation. Furthermore, the change in the view of information and information technology has been accompanied by a change in the role of informational managers. Numerous managers believe that, in order to maintain a perspective on behalf of the whole organization, the structure responsible for information technology applications has to have a senior management presence, and bring together the needs of end-user departments and the services of information technology providers. Even though the information technology department is still, in many companies, in the development phase of its life cycle, the evolution of a new breed of senior level managers, CIOs, is an indication of the endorsement by corporate executives of information technology as a vital strategic tool.

An early article speculating about the impact of information technology on organizations was written in 1958 by Robert Slater, a manager who had just completed one of the large-scale applications of computer systems to insurance office operations. Slater predicted, among other things, a shift of operations to the then-called electronic data processing (EDP) department and more power and influence of the data processing (DP) executive (Slater 1958).

When one examines the design and structure of U.S. corporations, the reality remains that information management is one of the less than efficiently managed key elements of any company. One of the criticisms of the way organizations manage information technology is the fact that the top IT manager is usually in a staff role; "the further you get from the people who have control of the operations of the company on a daily basis, the less impact you have," (CIO 1990: 39). A number of companies, however, are realizing this pitfall and making information management a line position to the greatest degree possible, motivated by the belief that the IT manager in a line function will contribute directly to the accomplishment of the objectives of the organization. In addition, many corporations have come to grips with the fact that if information technology is to play a vital strategic role, then the IT manager is to be an active player at the top and report directly to the CEO or the CFO. Even though most CEOs do not have the IT function reporting directly to them now, they probably will within a few years.

Promoting IT managers to corporate or executive positions reporting to the CEO or the CFO reflects a recognition of the strategic value of information technology to the organization. No matter how else the company attempts to support the matching process between information and information technology and building competitive advantage, the top IT executive must be included in the "inner circle" of senior management for two critical reasons: (1) to communicate the strategic potentials and limitations of information technology to senior management and (2) to avoid the filtering of senior management business objectives through several layers before reaching the IT department (Guimaraes, Farrell, & Song 1988). In other words, the time and effort spent in officer meetings to discover the common ground between the IT officer and the business officers put the company on firmer ground when it comes to making strategic IT investments that truly reflect business priorities. Recently, many IT managers have invested much energy into transforming their function from service providers to strategic partners with the business.

To accomplish this end, many large companies have created a senior executive position on the corporate level, a CIO. The CIO is a top management executive position with the responsibility for managing information and information technology's critical corporate resources from a global company-wide perspective. The creation of the CIO position is one way to manage information and information technology investments better.

Individuals handling CIO positions are not just technocrats; they are executives who have the competence, both technical and managerial, to straddle the historic gulf between the nontechnical people in the board room and the information technology managers from the data processing departments. Notwithstanding the fact that the CIO is the rookie of big-time corporate management, he or she has to be prepared to challenge the quality of the strategic thinking of the executive team, of which he is a member. These days, more and more nontechnical managers are filling this top information technology position; this movement has been going on since about 1975. As a matter of fact, many organizations considered the top IT post as a nontechnical post for many years. The San Francisco-based McKesson Corporation is an example of such an organization. In such organizations, the CIO is thought of in terms of critical success factors, a strategic planning concept applied to organizations by John Rockart of MIT. An important critical success factor for CIOs is to shift the IT organization's mind-set. It is necessary to move the organization from an attitude that is going to solve users' problems alone to a willingness to feel users out about their problems and work in tandem with them to solve the problem. A CIO must be able to facilitate innovation throughout the company. The power to lead, influence, and change is another critical success factor for any CIO. Another critical success factor is for the CIO to be able to move the way of thinking in the corporation from "what the technology is" to "what the technology can do" (*Computerworld* June 1989). CIOs are always on the look out for ways to better harness the power of new information technology in order to slash cost, boost productivity, improve sales and marketing, and help design the organization's grand strategy. Essentially, the CIO is responsible for planning and architecturing a firm's information resources and for promoting information technology throughout the organization.

The fever of the CIO phenomenon has been catching on rapidly in corporate America. In 1984, a Diebold survey of 130 major corporations found that one-third had someone in the CIO function, up from 5 percent of the same corporations in 1979 (Synnott 1987). In a 1989 *Computerworld* survey of 103 CEOs and other top business leaders in the Fortune 1000, 85 percent agreed that IT holds the key to the competitive advantage for their organizations in the 1990s; 88 percent said they believe information technology will significantly change the way their companies do business in the next decade (*Computerworld* April 1989).

The CIO's responsibilities are continuing to evolve. In recent years, information technology executives have become more and more concerned with organizational issues, such as communications with management and users, absorption of technology by the corporation, and the ability of information technology to respond quickly to change. In other words, the concerns of the CIO seem to be moving beyond technology toward the impact on the people, processes, and products of the corporation (Passino & Severance 1988).

INFORMATION TECHNOLOGY AND CONTROL SYSTEMS

According to F. Warren McFarlan, professor of information systems at Harvard Business School, the story of how information and information technology have been used to exploit external competitive opportunities has been well reported and documented. What has not received enough attention is the equally dramatic but much less visible impact of the new technology on management control systems; "advances in electronic data processing and telecommunications are having a far-reaching impact on the internal structure and processes of organizations" (McFarlan 1987). The controlling function consists of actions and decisions managers undertake to ensure that actual results are consistent with desired results. Effective control requires three basic conditions: (1) *standards* that reflect the ideal outcomes, (2) *information* that indicates deviation between actual and standard results, and (3) *corrective action* for any deviations between actual and standard results. The logic is evident that information technology facilitates effective control. In any organization, managers are concerned that resources are productively deployed, job responsibilities properly stated, and various assignments adequately coordinated. To ensure that resources are used appropriately, managers develop structures and use processes, such as planning, monitoring, and reporting, to maintain control. With the advances in information technology, comprehensive control systems based on a global or corporate view are applied today.

A company's management control systems serve several purposes. They inform managers as to what resources are available and in use by the firm. They also assist in coordinating and integrating diverse segments of the organization. Finally, they allow management to gather information from all layers of the organization for devising strategic alternatives and operating decisions. The main objective of a management control system is to ensure that employees do what the company requires them to do, in purposeful ways. Such systems coordinate the planning of future activities and later measure performance against those plans, thereby providing an efficient means for performance appraisal of individual workers and operating units.

Organizations allocate the steps in the decision-making and control processes across managers. These steps are (1) *initiation* (generating alternative ways to use resources), (2) *ratification* (the choice of decision alternatives), (3) *implementation* (executing the choices), and (4) *monitoring* (measuring and rewarding performance). The steps of initiation and ratification are called decision management. Decision control includes implementation and monitoring (Fama & Jensen 1983). Informational systems and information technology act as the linking pins among those four elements. They help in the coordination of the four activities, especially in the implementation and monitoring phases.

Control systems are either formal or informal. There are a number of classic-formal informational control systems employed in corporations, such as budgeting and boards of directors, and informal ones, such as managerial supervision. Further, as argued later in this book, the degree to which the control function is exercised by both top management and the board of directors depends on some organization-specific factors, such as the ownership structure of the corporation and the number of outside directors. It is one of the objectives of this book to show empirically that the presence of a CIO, as a management control agent, on the top management team is related directly, or indirectly, to such organization-specific factors.

INFORMATION TECHNOLOGY AND GLOBALIZATION

Economic globalization has affected information management in unexpected ways. The rapid growth of multinational corporations (MNCs) in both number and degree of influence has been accompanied by an unprecedented flow of information across international borders. The American Express company, for instance, authorizes more than 250,000 credit-card transactions daily from around the world, at an average rate of five seconds or less (*Business Week* 1983). This sort of globalization of information has raised questions about privacy protection and national sovereignty. Some nations, such as Brazil, have responded with regulations that threaten to interfere with the timely and efficient flow of information from one branch of an MNC to another. Other countries are even considering taxes and tariffs on corporate data flowing across their borders.

Over the past few years, a number of international conferences have addressed the impact of information technology on the economies and societies of industrially developed economies. The major discussions in those meetings have generally centered on the effect of IT on employment, industrial structure, telecommunications systems, and trade services. Some of those problems have been identified as having global implications. Attention, however, has focused on the impact of IT on smaller economic units and regional industries.

The economic impact of the information technology revolution is beginning to surface significantly on the global front. As a result, many developed countries have developed or are in the process of developing national IT policies. West Germany, for instance, is taking drastic steps to restructure its information technology industry to make it more competitive domestically and abroad, and compatible with its overall economic policy. Another example is Japan, where IT policy is based on two different understandings of the role of information technology in general. The first considers IT policy as an integral component of a microecomonic "industry" policy, and the second looks at IT from a broader social view. Fundamentally all observers agree that the introduction of IT policies on the global front will inevitably facilitate the utilization of information technologies more efficiently and productively.[1]

One of the global consequences of IT, however, is the international concern about the risks and dangers that industrial societies may face in the wide application of IT. One such risk may be found in the process of dehumanization that may accompany the wide diffusion of IT (Ogura 1989). Regardless of what has been stated, the international repercussions of corporate information and information technology promise to remain an uncertain and sensitive issue for the foreseeable future.

THE RESEARCH QUESTION AND HYPOTHESES

The main research question investigated by this study is as follows: What are the company-specific characteristics that act as determinants in the creation of a CIO position, on the one hand, and the level of investments in and performance of IT, on the other?

This question seems to be of a fundamental nature, since its answer will determine the relevance of an important managerial phenomenon: The relevance of a CIO position and the vitality of IT investments. Many companies take the position of "follow the leader" with respect to these two phenomena.

To answer the major research question, a number of hypotheses were formulated. These are:

H01a: Equity ownership by managers is negatively related to the creation of a CIO position on the top-level management team.

H02a: There exists a positive relationship between the creation of a CIO position on the top management executive team and the ratio of outside to inside directors on the board.

H03a: There exits a positive relationship between CEO duality in the corporation and the creation of a CIO position on the top-level management team.

H04a: There exists a positive relationship between the size of the firm and the creation of a CIO position on the top-level executive management team.

H05a: There exists a positive relationship between capital intensity and the creation of a CIO position on the top-level executive management team.

H06a: There exists a positive relationship between the technological level of the industry and the creation of a CIO position on the top-level executive management team.

H01b: Companies with relative IT advantage tend to have high equity ownership by managers.

H02b: Companies with relative IT advantage tend to have a higher ratio of inside to outside directors.

H03b: There exists a positive relationship between the size of the firm as measured by gross fixed assets and the company's relative IT index.

The first six hypotheses concerning the existence of a CIO position will be analyzed and tested in Chapter 4 of this book, whereas the three hypotheses pertaining to IT levels of investment and performance will be the subject of Chapter 5.

OVERVIEW OF METHODOLOGY

As will be discussed in detail in a later chapter, this research uses two different types of analysis and two different methods of data collection. As stated earlier, an empirical examination is conducted to determine significant organizational variables that are useful in explaining the phenomenon of creating a CIO position on the top-level executive management team that is used as a proxy for management recognition of the importance of information technology, on the one hand, and the level of investment in and performance of information technology, on the other. Specifically, an experiment is designed to test the two sets of hypotheses listed in the previous section. A cross-sectional design is used to compare corporations that had a CIO on the top-level management executive team in 1988 to corporations that did not have one for the same year. Data needed for this portion of the research were collected from public sources available from companies' proxies and annual reports. Where possible, these data were cross-validated from the proxies against information provided by *standard and Poor's Industrial Guide* and *Moody's Industrial Manual*. Data needed to test the set of hypotheses dealing with the level of investment in and performance of information technology were collected by means of a questionnaire/ survey of a number of Fortune 500 companies administered by the author.

Both univariate and multivariate statistical analyses will be employed to test the two sets of hypotheses. The t-test statistical technique was deemed necessary because the dependent variable is binary: a company with a CIO or without a CIO. The multivariate analysis employed is the logistics regression analysis. As will be explained in detail in Chapter 4, the logistic regression model (logit) was selected because the dependent variable is discrete (binary) and because logit analysis avoids some of the strong assumptions of multivariate analysis techniques, like discriminant analysis and multiple linear regression analysis (e.g., the independent variables are normally distributed and there is equality of the variance-covariance matrix).

The functional logistic regression equation was constructed as follows:

$$Y = F \text{ (MO, GA, RE, EM, OBD, CI, DU, IS)} \qquad (1.1)$$

where

Y	=	1 if the firm has a CIO
Y	=	0 if the company does not have a CIO
MO	=	management ownership
GA	=	book value of gross assets

RE   =   total revenues
EM   =   number of employees
OBD   =   ratio of outside to inside directors on the board
CI   =   capital intensity of firm
DU   =   duality of the CEO
IS   =   industry technological structure.

The size of the firm is measured by three proxies: book value of gross assets, total revenues, and number of employees. All other characteristics identified from the hypotheses will measured with one variable.

To test the hypotheses concerned with the performance of IT investments, an index is developed by the author, the relative information technology index (ITI), which will be used as a proxy for the different levels of IT performance. This index is developed in Chapter 5 later in this book.

ABOUT THE BOOK

Information technology and management control uses a theory-based, empirical investigation to describe the linkage between investment in and management of IT and the control of the organization which in turn is motivated by the management ownership structure. It specifically addresses the question of principal-agent relationship and the need for information systems and information technology to enhance this relationship; further, it investigates and explores those company-specific characteristics that influence top-level management to invest heavily in information technology.

The book is in six chapters. Chapter 1 provides an overview of the entire book and establishes the context for the research. Chapter 2 takes the reader through the impact of information technology on organizational structure and control systems. The issue of centralization versus decentralization is addressed, and the role IT plays in management decision to adopt one structure or another is examined. This chapter also provides a review of the literature on the role of information technology as a control "agent."

Chapter 3 covers the literature on agency theory and management ownership. In addition, it examines the different information systems employed by organizations, including the board of directors. The role of outside board members to assure efficient control is stressed, and the need for information technology in facilitating both the role of management and the board is also explored.

Management of information technology and the role of the CIO as a "safety net" for management control are covered in Chapter 4. The various methods, data collection, and sampling procedures are also discussed in this chapter, along with the set of hypotheses to be tested.

Chapter 5 is devoted to covering the questionnaire used to collect data from a number of Fortune 500 companies, data explanation and tabulation, empirical analyses, and results. Chapter 6 covers the conclusion and recommendation for future research.

NOTE

1. For an interesting discussion of information technology policies in developed economies, see Snow & Jussawalla (1989).

2

Information Technology, Organizational Structure, and Control

No doubt major changes in information technology are profoundly affecting the people, processes, structures, and strategies of organizations. Improved communications capabilities and data accessibility are leading to systems integration of business processes across traditional functional, product, or geographic lines.

Many researchers have commented on the effects of computerization, automation, and information technology on organizational structure. In 1958, as rapidly growing companies hired droves of middle managers and decentralized decision making, Leavitt and Whistler (1958) wrote a controversial article predicting a reversal of that trend in the 1980s. Their prediction, which met with strong criticism, held that the combination of management science, and information technology would prompt a shrinkage of middle management ranks and greater recentralization.

Since the publication of this article, many studies have been undertaken to examine the relationship between information technology and organizational structure. The conclusions of such studies have been either contradictory or, at best, inconclusive. In their research, Seigmen and Karsh (1962) and Whisler (1970) support the centralization thesis by arguing that organizations should make use of information technology to centralize the decision-making process and eliminate middle management layers. Of course, advanced information technology might lead to more centralized organizational structure. High-level managers will have the capability of bypassing middle managers and directly accessing data from the operating floor, thus decreasing senior management's dependence on lower-level managers and allowing the former to make almost all key operational decisions, or at least monitor them.   Pfeffer and Leblebici (1977), Robey (1981), and Burlingame (1961), on the other hand, report either an increase in decentralization or an enhancement of current organizational structures with the increase in the utilization of information technology. Their argument centers around the fact that IT would provide timely and relevant information that would facilitate decentralized decision making and delegation of power.

Regardless of the inconsistent conclusions drawn by the studies mentioned above, there is an agreement among the authors that information technology has many strategic and structural impacts on the ways companies are organized and controlled, specifically, how information technology affects the effectiveness of employees, the productivity of communications and interactions, and, ultimately, the overall growth and direction of companies at the macro level.

Sophisticated information technologies are changing the way we look at organizational structures. This is specifically pronounced in the widespread use by management personnel of personal computers that can tap into large centralized data bases and that are linked together as part of a larger computer network. The result is a wider span of control, fewer levels in the hierarchy, and lower complexity. Information technology may also lead to less formalization in organizations. The reason is that management information systems can substitute computer control for rules and decision discretion. Since computer technology can rapidly warn top management of the effects of any decision, however, it enables them to take corrective action if the decision is not to their liking. From the foregoing, we can conclude that even though information technology helps in the decentralization of the decision-making process, it does so with no commensurate loss of control by top management. This is sometimes referred to in the literature as the centralized-decentralized structure.

McFarlan and McKenney suggest that companies use information technology to change their organizational structure and management control policies for competitive advantage (McFarlan & McKenney 1983: 211). The two authors argue that in a competitive environment where cost minimization is critical, the use of information technology allows for greater utilization of the plant and reduces the inventory level. On the other hand, in an environment where product differentiation is critical, information technology will help shorten lead time for product development, or improve product customization features and provide an easy ordering system.

The remaider of this chapter is directed at examining the issues of the impact of IT on organizational structure, including the flattening of the hierarchy and the degree of centralization of the decision-making process. Then, the chapter examines the relationship between information technology and organizational performance. This is followed by a discussion of IT and strategic planning and IT as a control agent. The chapter wraps up with a concluding section.

THE FLATTENING OF U.S. ORGANIZATIONS

We are in an age of rapid technological development, compelling managers to redirect organizational efforts and redefine roles for a high-tech society. The most spectacular aspect of this era is the pervasive impact of information technology on organizational structure, management, planning, and control. If one considers businesses as subsystems in a whole system, one can easily observe that those economic entities are basically faced with two generic problems; the first is how to manage the internal components that have direct responsibility for the production of their products, and the second is how to interact with outside forces responsible for their survival, such as customers, regulatory agencies, competitors, both national and international, and the general socioeconomic trends in their surrounding environment. The most powerful explanation of why businesses invest in information technology and build sophisticated information systems, then, is to solve internal problems, improve internal efficiency, and respond to changing domestic and global environments.

As external and internal organizational factors change and organizational problems emerge, new technologies become essential, and old structures must be adjusted using these new technologies to be compatible with the changing environments. Consider, for instance, the impact that the unification of Europe into a single economic trading zone in 1992 is having on transnational informational systems of global and international companies. The European market of more than 320 million consumers with a $4 trillion combined economy will replace the United States as the largest single market in the world. Although 1992 promises an economic boom for Europe, both European, American, and Japanese companies are finding that vast change in their information technologies will be required. Quaker Oats Company is a case in point. This Chicago-based food products company has started developing "transnational" products like *Gatorade*, which is marketed in Italy, Canada, and Germany. To support the marketing of more transnational products, Quaker Oats is in the process of revamping its information technology infrastructure and rebuilding its systems to support common products sold to large geographic regions (*Information Week* Jan. 9, 1989).

Widespread implementation of information technology, however, creates two conflicting forces in most organizations. On the one hand, lower-level managers armed with data bases, terminals, microcomputers, and the like would have rapid access to a larger pool of information. With these tools, they are able to supervise, control, and direct activities considerably better, which, logically, would lead to centralized decision making. On the other hand, information technologies are being utilized to create large-scale centralized operations at the headquarters level. Robert Reich, one of the greatest public policy professors, states that the new organizational structure will dictate speed, flexibility, and the ability to customize output (Neubarth 1988). He also adds that the trend of the future is that more and more value added to a product consists of supplying customized information to customers. The recent move to link sales forces electronically to the organization in order to be more responsive to their customers is an example of such a trend.

Peter Drucker (1988) and Tom Peters (1988) have also sensed a necessity for organizational restructuring as a consequence of information technology. Both authors believe that the design of organizations is changing as a response to the widespread use of information technology, and stress that the organization of the future would have a strong emphasis on electronic networks that provide information flow within the organization as well as between the firm and its external constituents, such as customers, suppliers, shareholders, and so forth. In addition to the new structure, there will be a new corporate culture, telecommunications will be an absolute requirement for the functioning of the organization, and information resources would be managed at the strategic level by a chief information officer (Snyder & Zienert 1990: 128).

It is important here to recognize how information technology affects the confidence placed in the decisions made. By enabling top-level managers to obtain information quickly and accurately, information technology helps them make decisions that they, otherwise, may have been unwilling to make (Dawson & McLoughlin 1986).

Because of the profound impact of IT on organizational structure,

George Huber (1990) has raised the issue of the need to reinvestigate and possibly revise certain components of organizational theory. Huber argues that a large part of what is known about the factors affecting organizational processes, structures, and performance was developed when the nature and mix of information technologies were relatively constant, both across time and across organizations of the same general type (Huber 1990: 47). Although work and supervision are affected almost immediately when new information technologies are introduced, over a longer period of time the overall structure of organizations can change as well. Organizational structure is the interaction among the number of different levels in the organization, the type of work and workers involved, and the distribution of income.

The literature review of the impact of IT on organizational structure revealed that information technology is affecting organizational structure in two ways: First, many researchers and practitioners believe that information technologies are making organizations flatter by reducing the number of middle managers, and making organizations more efficient and productive. The leading proponent of this thesis is Peter Drucker (1980, 1988). Second, some have pointed out that because organizations now have extensive telecommunications technology, they no longer need the same number of employees. Instead, organizations can rely on outside contractors in an electronic marketplace to do the work, supervising them electronically and accepting or rejecting their work on a contractual basis (Laudon & Laudon, 1991).

The evidence to support these beliefs about information technologies' impact on organizational structure is still thin. Although information technologies have proved to be useful in producing letters, calculating spreadsheets, and printing lists of customers, this has not led to any wholesale decrease in white-collar jobs. As a matter of fact, information technologies have indeed had a powerful positive role to play in changing the strategy of businesses. Computer-based systems have revolutionized business procedures in some industries--notably retailing, financial services, and manufacturing. In addition, information technologies have helped to create new products, and they have contributed to the transformation of the U.S. economy into an information economy and will transform it in the near future into a knowledge economy.

CENTRALIZATION VERSUS DECENTRALIZATION

After a period in which many companies experimented with decentralizing their information systems (IS) organization, the pendulum is swinging back once again. Companies are consolidating data centers, beefing up authority of their central staffs, and establishing company-wide technical standards and work procedures. The trend toward recentralization is being driven by three factors (Von Simon 1990): (1) the high cost of multiple data processing facilities, (2) the changing demographics of the information systems profession, and, (3) the emphasis on company-wide information systems that integrate business functions and support new business opportunities (Von Simon 1990: 158).

The exercise of power through concentration or delegation of decision-making authority is still subject to conflicting judgments. Concentration improves reaction time to decisions that mandate changes in the strategic portfolio, of a company and enables tight coordination of activities among the various divisions and departments. Decentralization, on the other hand, allows flexibility with which departments and divisions can react to both internal and external environmental contingencies (Alexander & Fennell 1986).

During the last part of the 1980s, a number of companies adopted sophisticated telecommunications networks and centralized data bases, which integrated all aspects of highly centralized businesses. Senior managers started using these centralized data bases and networks to monitor and control their organizations, and to signal to employees the kinds of things they should focus on. This is a case where judgment is delegated downward but closely monitored by those above. In that case, there is no real sharing of control in the organization, and one could counter argue that there is only the appearance of decentralization and top-level management maintains effective centralized control. With centralization comes the concentration of decision making at a single point in the organization. A high concentration implies a high centralization.

In the 1980s, a new structural phenomenon emerged that promised to improve firm efficiency and profitability: Corporations started to structure themselves along the lines of small, tribe-like entrepreneurial units. Since these large corporations could not operate simply as a collection of independent tribes, they required a corporate infrastructure to integrate and align team efforts with the overall direction of the corporation. Information technology is making this integration possible (Vincent 1989).

The potential cost savings from recentralization are causing even those companies deeply committed to business unit independence to consolidate data centers, and centralize their IT resources and decision making. As the cost of communicating with mainframe at a remote site drops, it becomes less necessary to have multiple data centers near local business offices.

Probably the most important force driving the trend toward recentralization is the growing reliance on integrated information systems. No matter what the business, getting the market faster requires closer links among design, production, and service activities.

Another major reason for the move toward recentralization of information technology is the involvement of senior executives and line managers in using the technology. No longer willing to delegate the strategic or tactical uses of this technology to the information systems department, these managers are taking the lead in applying information technology to the most important areas of their businesses. Many are using the technology as a core element in aggressive new approaches to the marketplace and to enhance control of internal operations (Rockart 1988).

Examples that depict the move toward recentralization abound. The investment firm Merrill Lynch (New York) and the nation's sixth-largest bank (Los Angeles) have reverted to centralized management of their information technology departments. This move was part of the management-by-results (MBR) program both companies initiated in 1987. Under such a program, the IT department and end-users jointly conceive, build, and own strategic goals. This written contract predetermines productivity measures and shares rewards (Carlyle 1987).

In 1987, Hewlett Packard Company's (HP) corporate structure changed from one of divisional autonomy and entrepreneurship to a type of centralized management. Since then, this change has brought certain improvement in HP's ability to bring products to market.

Information technology is utilized by companies to thrive in an environment of fierce international competition, trade-barrier battles, and rapid technological advances. Part of the reason that Texas Instrument Company (TI) survived the volatile changes of the 1980s is that it created a global network that gave 76,000 employees equipped with 55,000 workstations access to data bases residing on 43 IBM mainframes in 20 data centers around the world.

General Signal Corporation, a diversified manufacturing firm with 28 autonomous units, had never centralized much of anything until March 1987, when it decided to create a central utility to sell information services to its business units. This has been far from the norm for such a decentralized firm. Although each subsidiary is still free to choose its own IT destiny, the General Signal Services utility has convinced most of them to sign on because of its economies of scale, additional CPU capacity and the elimination of data center operation worries (*Computerworld* Sept. 11, 1989: 1 and 16).

Ameritech, a Bell holding company, is working to centralize and standardize the information technology and information systems of its five telephone companies--Illinois, Wisconsin, Indiana, Michigan, and Ohio Bell. Officials believe that this five-year endeavor will reduce the company's long-term information processing costs by an impressive 20 percent (*Computerworld* April 30, 1990: 63-67).

Trailer Train Company, which supplies 65 percent of the flat cars used in North America, is in the process of centralizing its information systems, by hooking the company's 60 remote sites to the headquarter's host computer in Chicago. This would effectively take the organization from a decentralized to a centralized computer environment. The move toward a centralized computing environment falls in steps with Trailer Train's overall corporate philosophy of a centralized structure (*Computerworld* June 25, 1990: 67-70). (1) It is more economical, (2) the company will be able to provide more effective support, (3) efficiency in decision making is increased, and, (4) flexibility to make change is enhanced.

Westinghouse Communications Systems in Pittsburgh is charged with providing telecommunications and data services to Westinghouse business units. To implement the links, the credit company is relying on a nationwide network that Westinghouse is building for all of its subsidiaries. This network is only one of Westinghouse's strategies for consolidating its various internal networks. Chrysler is another company that has slowly but surely nudged its IT environment toward one in which users in various parts of the company could have easy and quick access to information generated in totally separate divisions. This allows a marketing department to have instant access to the latest work of the design department. About eight years ago, Chrysler began looking for a way to permit more data sharing among the various departments, and the Loosely Coupled Network (LCN) provided the means. Although making the LCN tool work well required significant effort, the benefit to Chrysler Corporation was quick in coming.

In 1989, Lockheed corporation merged its aircraft facilities in California and Georgia, consolidating their IT groups. In 1987, Corning Glass Works, Inc. centralized control of its corporate information services through implementing a computer networking strategy that unified and built on the strengths of the company's IBM and Digital Equipment Corporation environments. The networking strategy helped Corning improve connectivity between scattered corporate facilities, improve network performance, and cut costs by maximizing existing telecommunications facilities.

Corporate data centers are coming under closer scrutiny as part of a general trend toward cost control in U.S. business. Data center operations represent 50 percent to 70 percent of the information technology budget and are growing. The people at the top of corporations start to consider how to cut back on expenses. Among the more publicized cost-cutting efforts were the disclosure in January of 1990 that AT&T was moving to consolidate its data centers operations from 12 sites into five, and the 1989 decision of Eastman Kodak Company to outsource three major components of its information processing operations and consolidate its data center operations from four to one (Polilli, July 1990: 23-25). Information systems executives at both companies say that consolidation and outsourcing will accomplish far more than just cost reduction. Both strategies, in fact, are as much techniques for improving the quality of information services and instituting greater management control as they are for reducing expenses.

Although cost pressures and technological changes have led to the reevaluation of data center operations at several firms, mergers and acquisitions have also contributed to a duplication of effort in some IT organizations. In 1988, TI completed the centralization of its world wide electronic data interchange (EDI) operations in order to make it easier for its trading partners to deal with its many business units and to encourage new partners to participate in its EDI network. The major internal applications that are EDI-ready are purchasing, traffic, marketing, shipping, accounts receivables, and accounts payable. This centralization of EDI has proven to cut operations cost, reduced data entry errors, and improved management control over the different facets covered. This centralized EDI network contains 38,000 terminals and desktop computers, 1,250 minicomputers, and 40 mainframes in 17 countries (*Network World* April 4, 1988: 2, 8).

In 1984, General Motors Corporation (GM) announced a massive change in its organizational structure. GM set about to create two major automotive divisions out of the multi division structure it has had for half a century. In addition, GM added Electronic Data Systems to the corporate field to begin building a corporate-controlled artificial intelligence operation (*Business Week* July 16, 1984). These changes represent a move toward intensified corporate control and centralized automotive design and manufacture.

The banking industry is being reshaped with "mega-banks" created through mergers and acquisitions that gather a tremendous number of financial services for centralized team management. During the deregulation era of the early 1980s, mergers and acquisitions resulted in fewer but larger bank groups with centralized data processing and electronic coordination of services (*Business Week*, June 18, 1984).

It is concluded then that the strategy of recentralizing information technology and decision making, in some of the larger corporations in the United States, is driven by a number of factors, the most important of which is greater management control. The way one looks at the cause-and-effect relationship between organizational structure and information technology is one of the very possible explanations for these inconsistent results (Sung 1988). There exist two basic conceptual models that underlie this relationship: the organization imperative and the technology imperative. The organization imperative looks at information technology as an outcome of managerial design choices aiming at creating a fit between the organization and its environment. The principle of the organizational imperative is that organizational outcomes are the results of intended rational managerial actions; that is, managers and systems designers have considerable influence over the choice of appropriate information technology to achieve their desirable objectives. Simon (1977) contends that managers can achieve desirable objectives and avoid negative consequences by making technology fit their needs. On the other hand, the technology imperative treats information technology as an exogenous factor, independent from the organizational variables that it affects. The technological imperative was embraced by Leavitt and Whisler (1958), who maintained that information technology led to structural recentralization and reduction in middle-level managers.

The trend shows that with the advances of information technology, corporations are moving in the direction of a centralized-decentralized structure; that is, business units are given the authority to make decisions under the close supervision of corporate management. This structure allows the latter to interfere when it sees fit, thereby preventing wrong decisions from being made and insulating the company from what is believed to be unsound judgments.

INFORMATION TECHNOLOGY AND PERFORMANCE

Businesses are investing tremendous amounts of money and human resources in IT. A 1985 study by Strassmann found that the average information technology expenditure in 1983 was 2 percent of revenues. Another study (Diebold Group, 1982, 1984) found that centralized management information technology expenditures on average accounted for 1.44 percent of revenues in 1984. For a Fortune 500 company of $10 billion, this expenditure amounts to $200 million per year, which is a respectable amount. More recently, Harris and Katz (1988) demonstrated that high-performing companies allocate a more significant proportion of their annual income to IT expenditures than companies with lower performance.

Measuring the impact of information technology on organizational performance is a difficult job to perform. For many organizations, the need to come up with an IT performance measure has become particularly important in recent years. As information technology assumes a more strategic role in companies, the ad hoc estimates of the past must be replaced by more systematic measures in the future (Singleton et al. 1988). The rampant character of many of the new information technologies now being adopted and the rapidly changing technologies that underlie these systems, however, serve to make this measurement task a more difficult one than those faced by many other parts of the business. The impact of IT on organizational performance will naturally vary from organization to organization and industry to industry. One thing is certain, though: Without systematic measurements, managers will have little to guide their actions other than experience and intuition. As organizations grow and become more complex and global in nature, however, it becomes increasingly more difficult to rely on intuition alone.

There is no one measure that covers all aspect of IT activities, just as there is no one measure that captures the complete picture of a firm's economic health. According to Singleton and colleagues, "What is needed is a set of measures, appropriate for the activity of objectives being measured."

A number of studies have investigated IT investments and their effect on performance. These studies have used a variety of measures of the level of investment in IT. The first of these studies is that conducted by the Diebold Group in 1982 and 1984. In a survey of major organizations over a ten-year period, Diebold used three quantities as proxies for the levels of information technology in an organization. These are: (1) management information system budget as a percentage of revenues, (2) management information system staff as a percentage of total staff, and, (3) ratio of hardware expenditures to personnel costs.

Datamation conducts and publishes surveys on a regular basis of the Fortune 1000 and 500 companies to estimate centralized management information system investment (Datamation 1986, 1987). The measure used by Datamation is the budget for the information system department as a percentage of revenues. In addition, several researchers have relied on proxy measures rather than absolute investment dollars for the purpose of comparing firms within one industry. Turner (1985), for instance, used a number of proxy measures, including the ratio of data processing expenditure to total asset and the number of standard functional areas having computerized applications.

According to Weill and Olson (1989), all of these approaches have advantages and disadvantages. It is uncertain, however, if any one of them captures all of a given company's investment in information technology because of the "increased centralization of IT investment and increasing ad hoc expenditures on IT from non-IT operational budget." (Weill & Olson 1989: 6).

As stated above, the measurement of IT performance is a highly complex process. A number of social and economic measures can be adopted (Zammuto 1982), and in fact, many combinations have been used in previous research. In studying the insurance industry, Bender (1986) used the ratio of the expenses over premium income as a measure of IT performance. However, other researchers contend that one single measure of performance is not representative of all the factors that contribute to high performance. Cron and Sobol (1986), in studying a sample of wholesalers, used four measures of performance: pretax income, return on assets, return on net worth, and five-year growth rates. Different performance measures were utilized by other researchers, including market share (PIMS Program 1984) and the ratio of net operating income to total asset base (Turner 1985).

In studying the impact of information technology on the performance of a sample of companies in the warehousing industry, Cron and Sobol found that those firms that made extensive use of information technology were either very strong or very weak financial performers.

Turner (1985) studied the performance of information technology in a sample of 58 savings banks. His research concluded that there was no statistically significant relationship between organizational performance and levels of investment in information technology.

Recently, Harris and Katz (1988) conducted a four-year study of 40 insurance companies. Their research reveals that the most profitable firms are more likely to spend a significantly higher proportion of their non interest operating expenses on IT. Any statement of causality in the study was not possible, leaving the question open of whether higher investment causes higher performance (Weill & Olson 1989: 7).

Weill and Olson conducted six mini case studies to help understand how firms define and manage information technology investments. They found that a wide variety of definitions and methods of measuring IT performance exist and that although firms acknowledge the importance of IT investment to organizational performance, they do not have a satisfactory way of assessing the relationship.

To define the relationship between information technology and organizational performance, some comprehension of the organization, its structure, goals, and objectives is imperative since each firm has its organizational-specific characteristics. Each organization has a different way of interacting with its inner and outer environments, and has a particular relationship with its customers and suppliers.

Later in Chapter 5, a relative IT index will be developed by the author to measure the impact of IT investment on performance. This index is believed to be an appropriate indicator of IT performance.

INFORMATION TECHNOLOGY AND STRATEGIC PLANNING

Organizations have been using information technology to support and strengthen their business strategies. The strategic concerns that information technology managers face relate to the increased importance of the use of information technology in the workplace. Just defining the job of the chief information officer is an issue corporate executives in our day are struggling with.

Information is a valuable asset of the organization. The more useful the information, the more valuable it is. The most relevant information the organization needs is that information needed for strategic decisions in the organization. Strategic decisions are those major decisions that affect the long-term direction of the organization: Decisions to expand into new markets, develop a new product, or finding a new niche in the market are all examples of strategic decisions.

A framework developed by John Rockart (1979) states that

information needs *and consequently information technology needed* [author's italics] can be derived from critical success factors, in other words, the key areas for any organization in which performance must be satisfactory if the business is to survive and thrive. Critical success factors (CSFs) differ among industries and for individual firms within a particular industry. The Rockart research team at MIT has identified four primary sources of CSFs: (1) industry-based factors; (2) competitive strategy, industry position, and geographic location; (3) environmental factors; and (4) temporal factors. The critical success factors method has been used by organizations as a means for determining their strategic directions. Executives as well as functional managers identify those five or six factors that are critical to the achievement of the organization's objectives.

Information technology has changed the practice of strategic competition in three directions. First, innovations in information technology are altering the structure of industries. New companies are surfacing that could be characterized as being vertically disaggregated, relying on other companies for manufacturing, marketing, distribution, and so on. Some authors think that these information-based networks, which are working on a contractual basis with other firms, may represent the future organizational model for corporations. The network organizational model, if adopted, would be only the third real innovation since the mid-1880s, when vertically integrated firms were set up. The other two changes were the divisional structure, in which the vertical chain of command for each operating division existed in parallel, and the "matrix" system, in which employees reporting to various supervisors made it easier to assemble temporary teams for big projects (Krommenacker 1989: 125). Second, information technology is an increasingly important lever that companies can use to create strategic competitive advantage through enhanced differentiation strategies, lower costs, and/or a change in scope. Finally, information technology is generating completely new businesses by making them technologically and economically feasible, in other words, by creating new businesses from within existing ones (Porter & Miller 1985).

Information technology, then, can bring a significant strategic competitive advantage to the firm. In addition to the cost savings incurred, benefits center on increased customer loyalty, tighter connections to customers, rapid response to customer needs, and increased product differentiation. Some of the more specific impacts on the competitive nature of the organization include increased efficiency, lower inventory costs, higher sales, and immediate feedback on product availability and price. In this low-cost, efficient climate, companies are looking for strategic opportunities. Commonly recognized companies that have used information technology to compete strategically include American Airlines, which changed industry structure and the rule of competition with their reservations system; Digital Equipment Corporation (DEC), which uses information technology to configure computer systems to their customers at a minimum cost; and Western Union, which generated new businesses using its communications network to provide message services for personal computers, word processors, and other electronic devices.

Evaluating environmental trends, both at the macro and micro levels, is one of the key areas of concern for any strategic manager. Information technology has proven to be of tremendous value in accomplishing this task. The increased flow of data and information between the company and its constituents provides an earlier detection of market shifts, gives a more accurate picture of competitor capabilities, and improves ability to predict customer reactions to the company's products.

Information technology has been demonstrated to be instrumental in helping businesses pursue the four competitive strategies (Laudon & Laudon 1991):

* Low-cost leadership: production at lower prices than competitors
* Focus on market niche: create new market niche
* Product differentiation: develop unique new products
* Develop tight linkages to customer and suppliers that "lock" them into the firm's products.

Each of these strategies provides a general framework within which a firm sets functional policies and procedures, and performs activities that implement that strategy. If a firm executes one of these strategies successfully, it will enjoy an advantage relative to its competitors and will yield higher than average return (Parsons 1983).

The first three approaches for strategic business systems emanate from the work of Michael Porter. Porter identified five competitive forces with which companies must contend: (1) the threat of new entrants into one's industry, (2) the bargaining power of buyers, (3) the bargaining power of the supplier, (4) the availability of substitute products or services, and (5) the intensity of rivalry among competitors (Porter 1985). To deal interactively with these competitive forces, a company would pursue one or more of the following three strategies. The first of these strategies is the cost leadership. Firms following an overall cost leadership strategy will utilize information technology to reduce the cost of their products by increasing efficiency in most functional areas ranging from engineering to manufacturing. For example, L'eggs Brands, Inc., a major hosiery company, developed a manufacturing and control inventory system in 1988 to reduce inventory and cut manufacturing costs by closely coordinating inventory and production requirements. In addition, L'eggs was able to eliminate inventory in warehouses by coordinating production plans tightly with sales, and thereby reducing its total cost and being able to compete on low prices.

The second business strategy is differentiation. Companies following differentiation strategies will utilize information technology to add unique features to their products. Information technology can support a differentiation strategy in a variety of ways: better customer service, better product design, better access to markets. The third strategy is market focus. This strategy entails the focus on a segment of a product line or a geographical niche that other companies do not serve. Porter indicates that these strategies may be used in combination; that is, the firm may choose to be a low-cost producer of a differentiated product.

Information technology has also been used to lock in customers through increasing the "switching" costs of those customers, in other words, making it costly and inconvenient for them to switch to a competitor. An example of a company that successfuly locked in customers is American Hospital Supply, which locked in its customers electronically through a computer network. Creating relationships with suppliers that maximize the firm's purchasing power is another application of information technology. Major U.S. auto companies have established electronic links with major suppliers. The Chrysler Corporation, for instance, is linked electronically to the Budd Company of Rochester, Michigan, a leading supplier of sheet metal parts, wheel products, and frames. The latter pulls manufacturing releases from Chrysler terminals installed in all of its work areas. Chrysler secures savings from strict delivery requirements that specify parts to be supplied on the day they are needed (Laudon & Laudon 1991: 59).

Other strategic issues facing information managers is making the IT department compatible with corporate planning. According to Sprague and McNurlin (1986), several planning frameworks can help information technology managers. These are:

* To evaluate their level of use of particular technologies
* To determine what few critical success factors are important
* To classify which parts of the organization are being supported by IT and which ones are not
* To study their expenditures on information technology from an investment point of view (Sprague & McNurlin 1986: 487).

INFORMATION TECHNOLOGY AS A CONTROL AGENT

The word control suggests the operations of checking, testing, regulation, verification, and adjustment (Holt 1990: 593). As a management function, control is the process of taking the necessary corrective action to ensure that the organization's mission and objectives are accomplished as effectively and efficiently as possible in keeping the stockholders' welfare as the number one priority.

Information is a source of organizational dependence. The people who control information are in a position to comprehend phenomena and focus on the solutions. "The more detailed and operational the information, the more closely they are able to supervise the activities in question" (Linder 1989: 53).

Many American corporations today are dependent on information technology for their survival and success. Information technology lays the foundation in the coordination of various departments and different teams and groups. Information technology can also be used for competitive advantage. Computer-integrated manufacturing, robotics, and statistical quality control are key elements of enhancing managerial control. As a control agent, information technology has also been utilized to form distribution channels, establish coordinating links in multi-firm value-added chains, and provide features to differentiate products.

Information technology is closely related to control, since advanced information systems allow a faster and more flexible responses to changing conditions. In addition, the communication potential of information technology allow data to be transmitted to any point in the organization regardless of the geographic dispersion of the different units of the organization. Buchanan and Boddy (1983) maintain that "as the purpose of information handling is usually to affect control in some respect, control technology is perhaps a more appropriate label then information technology" (p. 38). Other management researchers view information technology as the technology of control or an agent of control; among those are Whisler, Pfeffer, and Leblebici. The authors assert that information technology affects organizational structure through its impact on organizational control requirements and mechanisms.

The relationship between technology, in general, and control has been discussed by Woodward (1970) and Ovalle (1984). Woodward studied the relationship between technology and organizational design. In her research, she states that "control may be an intervening variable between technology and industrial behavior" (p. 39).

One problem in studying organizational control is that control and structure have not been clearly distinguished in organization theory literature. Thompson (1967) suggests that it is the need for the control and coordination that accompany technology, that has the direct impact on structure. Also, Reeves and Woodward (1970) argue that the core technology is of interest only because it influences the control needs of organizations, and theorists should therefore study the relationship between control and structure. In summary, each perspective starts with examining technology and structure, and each comes to the conclusion that it is the control needs of technology that affect organizational structure.

Outchi (1977) was one of the pioneers in separating control from structure by stating that structure consists of the familiar variables of centralization, formalization, specialization, and differentiation

Control means assuring that the principal's actions and work get done by some people. Control has two features, strategic and operational, and both are required for control to be effective. The size and complexity of most corporations have necessitated the incorporation of multilevel, multidimensional organizational control systems. These control systems are categorized into either strategic, long-term control systems, or operational, short-term control systems. Strategic control systems focus on issues of competitive advantage. Modern information technology is dramatically improving the quality of strategic control.

Information technology has been used essentially to enhance internal control, both operational and strategic. In addition, IT has been utilized to improve external control of the organization over the several factors in its external environment, such as monitoring competition activities, market mechanisms, and so forth.

SUMMARY

The purpose of this chapter was to present an examination of how information technology has affected organizations and management. For most of the past 25 years, the role of information technology was to save operational and administrative costs; the job of the data processing manager has been to manage information systems professionals and support transaction processing. The impact of information technology on organizational structure was not studied until recently. The literature reviewed in this chapter examined the impact of IT on organization structure. In a nutshell, IT has caused U.S. organizations to become leaner and flatter. The mania of downsizing and the elimination of a number of layers from the organizational hierarchy are caused mainly by the introduction of information technology in the workplace. In addition, thousands of middle-level management positions are being eliminated.

In our day, information technology executives find themselves in the spotlight. They are being expected to help improve the efficiency of the workplace by increasing the productivity of the various departments, through the use of information technology. They are looked at to improve the competitive position of their organizations by developing strategic IT systems and help improve division-to-division communications by linking all organizational sites with an integrated telecommunications network.

3

Information Technology, Agency Theory, and Control

This chapter is divided into six sections. The first section presents a brief examination of agency theory, its concepts, foundation, and notable development over the years. Section two presents a discussion of the underlying theoretical relationship among control, agency, and information technology. It is argued that, on the one hand, the size and complexity of most corporations have necessitated the incorporation of multilevel, multidimensional organizational control systems. On the other hand, size and complexity have contributed to increasing agency costs and to an overflow of information. One of the means utilized to decrease agency costs and improve efficiency of the control systems in an organization is the employment of information technology. Section three examines the relationship between agency theory and management ownership, on one hand, and management ownership and control, on the other. It is maintained that share ownership by a firm's managers is considered to be one element that reduces agency costs. This is perfectly logical since managers' losses caused by their less-than-optimal behavior is larger if their share ownership is greater.

Section four investigates the importance of information in agency theory. Information and incentives are the roots of agency theory, in which people are assumed to be rational, maximizing individuals who do not have the same information in that either action or knowledge can be hidden. Consequently, the agency problem will arise. The following section explores the role of the board of directors as an information system. Agency theorists view the board of directors as a mechanism for reducing agency cost arising from the problem of separation of ownership (risk bearing) and control (management) in a corporation. The board of director is viewed as a means of controlling the non-value-maximizing behavior of management. From an agency perspective, then, boards can be used as monitoring devices for shareholders' interests. The last section summarizes the chapter and sets the ground for Chapter 4.

AGENCY THEORY: THE LITERATURE

A significant body of literature dealing with agency relationship has evolved over the last decade or so. Agency theory was first developed by Jensen and Meckling in 1976. Its framework is concerned with the contractual relationship of stockholders, managers, and employees in an organization. In general, stockholders are treated as principals and managers are treated as agents.

Agency theory is concerned with resolving two problems that can occur between principals and agents. The first is referred to as the agency problem, which occurs when (a) it is difficult for the principal to verify what the agent is doing, and/or (b) the goals and objectives of the principals and agents conflict. The second is the problem of risk sharing, which occurs when the principal and agent have different attitudes toward risk. Because the principal and agent have different risk preferences, they would prefer different courses of action (Eisenhardt 1989: 58).

Agency models have been developed to examine the relationship that exists when one party (the agent) is engaged to act on behalf of another (the principal). The origin for agency theory is the separation of control and ownership in large corporations. Further, the existence of asymmetric information provides incentives for agents to use their superior information strategically to their personal advantage. Recently, there has been much work on the impact of informational asymmetries on allocation of economic welfare.

In agency theory, it is assumed that both principals and agents are rational, economic individuals who act in their own self-interest. A conflict will occur between agents and principals because of individual self-interest. For example, agents (managers) attempt to maximize their own interests. Consequently, principals (equity holders or debt holders) do not optimize their interests, and "agency costs" are incurred. An agency cost is the reduction in the owner-manager's utility, and/or the cost of the agency relationship between the managers and the outside shareholders or the managers and the debt holders. There are two types of agency costs. The agency costs of equity are the direct costs due to the stockholder-manager conflict. These include perquisite consumption by managers, monitoring and bonding costs from hiring outside monitors, and the cost resulting from non-optimal investment policy. According to the recent agency theory literature, the agency costs of equity are assumed to be a function of managerial ownership, leverage, and dividends. As managerial ownership, leverage, and dividends increase, equity ownership will decrease.

The agency costs of debt include the direct costs from the stockholder-bondholder conflict, reduced bond prices from possible managerial risk shifting, monitoring and bonding costs, and costs from underinvestment. The agency literature assumes that bond agency costs are a function of managerial ownership, leverage, and dividends. The greater the managerial ownership, the lower the bond agency costs. On the other hand, as leverage and dividends increase, so do bond agency costs.

Agency theory recognizes that because common stockholders are dispersed and hold well-diversified portfolios, they delegate responsibilities and decision making to corporate managers. These stockholders care primarily about diversifying away company's risks, whereas managers have an inclination to pursue their own interests, which might conflict with those of the stockholders giving rise to equity agency cost (Crutchley & Hansen 1989).

Several ways have been suggested to reduce equity agency costs. One way is for managers to increase their common stock ownership of the firm, better aligning their interests with stockholders' interests (Jensen & Meckling 1976). Equity agency cost will be reduced to zero, if managers own 100 percent of the corporation. However, as managers increase their ownership of the corporation, their wealth becomes poorly diversified, which in turn increase their personal risk. To counterbalance this increase in their risk level, managers will require increasing amounts of compensation.

Easterbrook (1984) suggests increasing dividends as another way of reducing equity agency cost. When larger dividends are paid, the chance that external equity capital will have to be raised will increase, and this in turn leads to managers being monitored by the Exchanges, the Securities and Exchange Commission, investment bankers, and providers of new capital. This monitoring causes managers who seek to retain their employment to act more in line with stockholders' interests.

Another way to reduce equity agency costs is to use more debt financing (Jensen & Meckling 1976). This will reduce manager-stockholder conflict by decreasing equity financing. However, debt financing gives rise to what is called debt agency cost by creating a conflict of interest between stockholders and creditors.

Equity and debt agency cost diminish firm worth. To decrease these costs, managers can adopt the least costly financial policy by trading off the benefits and costs of personal stock ownership with the benefits and costs of debt financing, and with the benefits and costs of paying dividends (Crutchley & Hansen 1989).

CONTROL, AGENCY, AND INFORMATION TECHNOLOGY

Control means assuring that the principal's actions and work are done by some people. Control has two features, strategic and operational, and both are required for control to be effective. The word control suggests the operations of checking, testing, regulation, verification, and adjustment (Holt 1990: 593). As a management function, control is the process of taking the necessary corrective action to ensure that the organization's mission and objectives are accomplished as effectively and efficiently as possible in keeping the stockholders' welfare as the number one priority.

Control, then, is the purpose of agency (White 1985: 187). Agency permeates the running of large, global corporations. Richard F. Vancil (1983) observed that a key feature of large, decentralized business corporations in this country is that "the group of managers in each firm is self-selected and self-perpetuating." Agency is the link between formal organization and markets (White 1985: 189). Organizational control is one of the most fundamental and most important areas of management activities, but possibly "one of the most neglected and least understood" management functions (Dauten et al. 1958: 42). Over the years, there have been vast dissimilarities in explanations of control among management theorists. McKinsey (1922) and Williams (1934) explicitly introduced the idea of contingency planning as a means of control. Their views of control centered around the financial aspects of the firm's operations, including accounting, budgeting, and interpretation. Fayol (1949) regards control as the primary function of management, in that it integrates the other management functions.

One problem in studying organizational control is that control and structure have not been clearly distinguished in organization theory literature. Thompson (1967) suggests that the need for control and coordination that accompanies technology, has the direct impact on structure. Also, Reeves and Woodward (1970) argue that the core technology is of interest only because it influences the control needs of organizations, and theorists should therefore study the relationship between control and structure. In summary, each perspective starts with examining technology and structure, and each comes to the conclusion that it is the control needs of technology that affect organizational structure.

Outchi (1977) was one of the pioneers in separating control from structure by stating that structure consists of the familiar variables of centralization, formalization, specialization, and differentiation

The size and complexity of most corporations have necessitated the incorporation of multilevel, multidimensional organizational control systems. These control systems are categorized into either strategic, long-term control systems, or operational, short-term control systems. Strategic control systems focus on issues of competitive advantage. Modern information technology is dramatically improving the quality of strategic control.

Control of the agency problem in the decision process is vital when decision makers (managers) are not the main shareholders. Under such circumstances, managers shoulder a small portion of the wealth effects resulting from their decisions, and they may be more likely to make decisions that are not in the best interests of the shareholders. The separation of decision management from decision control is utilized as a main mechanism by large corporations to reduce agency costs generated by the separation of control from ownership (Fosberg 1989). In the case where decision management and control are concentrated in the same entities, it would be fairly easy for these entities to engage in non-optimal behavior. Separating decision management from decision control "puts a set of checks and balances in the decision mechanism of the firm that makes it more difficult for the firm's managers to expropriate the wealth of the shareholders" (Fosberg 1989: 27).

If managers are to be accountable for their actions and the actions of their subordinates, and if they are to carry out their control responsibilities in an effective and efficient manner, they require ready access to current information concerning what, when, and how things have transpired in their spheres of influence. According to Child (1984), information technology strengthen managers' ability to control by communicating information rapidly across distances and by utilizing computational routines. In addition, he suggests that IT does not have an independent effect on work and organization; rather control consequences are the results of (1) decisions to select particular information processing capabilities, and (2) decisions as to how to use and develop these capabilities.

Managers, basically, have to protect their own interests as well as the interests of stockholders, and those who fail to anticipate, read, and respond to changes in their organization's vital signs will not be able to carry out their responsibilities well, if at all. Information technologies have been utilized to ensure that managers receive the appropriate information at the right time (Kreitner 1990). "The purpose of an MIS is to raise the process of managing from the level of piecemeal spotty information, intuitive guesswork, and isolated problem solving to the level of systems insights, systems information, sophisticated data processing, and systems problem solving" (Murdick & Ross 1977: 8).

Every information system has two intertwined components, one tangible, the other intangible (Clifton 1981: 28-37). The tangible part consists of all hardware and physical data records, whereas the "intangible portion is made up of human beings and their mental and communicative abilities" (Kreitner 1990: 646).

Being able to do more with less is probably the most common justification for the use of information technology in the control process. Perhaps the most valuable benefit of IT is the enhanced visibility and speed this technology provides to managers at all levels.

How information technology has been utilized to promote management control has not been well reported and capitalized on in the literature. Development in information technology, both of hardware and software, is having far-reaching consequences for the internal structure and mechanisms of organizations. The controlling function consists of actions and decisions managers undertake to ensure that actual results are consistent with desired results. The logic is evident that information technology facilitates effective control. In any organization, managers are concerned that resources are productively deployed, job responsibilities properly stated, and various assignments adequately coordinated. To ensure that resources are used appropriately, managers develop structures and use processes, such as planning, monitoring, and reporting to maintain control. With the advances in information technology, comprehensive control systems based on a global or corporate view are possible today.

A company's management control systems serve several purposes. They inform managers as to what resources are available and in use by the firm. They also assist in coordinating diverse segments of the organization. Finally, they allow management to gather information from all layers of the organization for devising strategic alternatives and operating decisions. A management control system attempts to ensure that people do what the company requires them to do, and in meaningful ways. Such systems coordinate the planning of future activities and later measure performance against those plans, thereby providing an efficient means for punishing or rewarding individual workers and operating units.

Organizations allocate the steps in the decision-making and control processes across managers. These steps are (1) *initiation* (generating alternative ways to use resources), (2) *ratification* (the choice of decision alternatives), (3) *implementation* (executing the choices), and, (4) *monitoring* (measuring and rewarding performance). The steps of initiation and ratification are called decision management. Decision control includes implementation and monitoring (Fama & Jensen 1983). Informational systems and information technology act as the linking pins among those four elements. They help in the coordination of the four activities, especially in the implementation and monitoring of activities.

Control systems are either formal or informal. There are a number of classic-formal informational control systems employed in corporations, such as budgeting and boards of directors, and informal ones, such as managerial supervision. Further, as argued later in this book, the degree to which the control function is exercised by both top management and the board of directors depends on some organization-specific factors, such as the ownership structure of the corporation and the number of outside directors. It is one of the objectives of this book to show empirically that the presence of a CIO, as a management control agent, on the top management team is related directly, or indirectly, to such organization-specific factors.

AGENCY THEORY AND MANAGEMENT OWNERSHIP

The extent of ownership and control separation was first examined by Berle and Means in 1932. Their study concluded that the control of a modern corporation was in the hands of hired managers rather than the owners. In their words, the modern corporation was characterized by "ownership of wealth without appreciable control and control of wealth without appreciable ownership" (p. 69).

Ever since Berle and Means published their essay on the separation of company's ownership and control, there has been a heated discussion on the importance of management ownership and the diversity of stockholders. If managers own all the stocks of the company, then they will bear the full cost of any value-reducing decisions. Consequently, there will be no equity agency costs. Further, if there are no debts outstanding, managers are the only owners of the firm; therefore, there will be no bond agency costs. In this situation, the total agency costs will be zero. However, in real-life situation, managers will not hold all of the stock because of wealth limitations and diversification benefits. Jensen and Meckling (1976) argue that, in this case, as outside ownership increases, total agency costs will rise. Further, they maintain that there is an optimal ownership structure of the firm.

Dispersion of stock ownership is a determinant of who controls the firm. As the shares become more widely held, top-level management has more latitude in making decisions without a stockholder with enough shares to make monitoring management practical. This absence of a dominant stockholder to participate actively in managing the firm allows professional managers to control the firm.

The separation of ownership and control in publicly held corporations has caused potential conflicts between the interests of professional managers and shareholders. Shareholders' interests lie in maximizing the value of the firm, whereas in running the company, managers might make nonoptimal decisions (from the shareholders' viewpoint) that will maximize their welfare. This divergence of managers' and shareholders' objectives will, in all likelihood, lead to serious conflicts in decisions regarding the future orientation of the company (Baysinger, Kosnik, & Turk 1991).

Share ownership by a firm's managers is considered to be one element that reduces agency costs. This is perfectly logical since managers' losses caused by their less-than-optimal behavior would be increased in proportion to the amount of their share ownership. Empirical research (See Demsetz 1983), however, has reached far less than satisfactory conclusions on this matter. Some authors have argued that the distribution of ownership is a determinant of efficiency and strategic development of firms (See Galbraith 1967; Morris 1964; Pfeffer & Salancik 1978, Williamson 1964); others contend that the distribution of ownership structure is unrelated to performance or strategic development (See Demsetz 1983; Demsetz & Lehn 1985; Fama 1983; Jensen & Meckling 1976).

Researchers in several disciplines have empirically addressed the agency issue. Some of these empirical studies have explained various phenomena from an agency perspective, including mergers and diversification (Amihud & Lev 1981), managerial resistance to takeover (Walking & Long 1984), representative versus corporate sales force (Anderson 1985), salary vs. commission (Eizenhardt 1985, 1988), type of transfer price (Eccles 1985), share price (Wolfson 1985), acquisitions and divestitures (Argawal & Mandelker 1987), payment of greenmail (Kosnik 1987), cost of equity (Barney 1988), and golden parachute contracts (Singh & Harianto 1989). In an empirical study involving 779 firms, Llyold, Jahera, and Goldstein (1984) tested the extent to which management ownership affects agency risk. Their results suggest that share ownership has no effect on the agency risk of the firm. Their findings are probably the result of the proxy used in measuring management ownership, which is the percentage of the firm owned by the largest shareholders. All that can really be concluded from their study is that agency risk of the firm is unaffected by the concentration of share ownership.

According to Fama (1980), although self-interest motivation exist in a firm, the welfare of the individual (management, shareholders, or bondholders) is dependent on the success or survival of the firm. Therefore, reduced conflict among the members of the firm might result in an increase in the welfare of some members without a decrease in the welfare of any of the others. This is the foremost reason why managers try to decrease agency costs, regardless of the extent of their share ownership. In addition, given a competitive managerial labor market, managers may make great effort to ensure the success and survival of the firm. Otherwise, managers will be subject to direct or indirect pressures from the sharcholders (Fama 1980: 292).

The research on the separation of ownership and control developed gradually, and the focus soon shifted from the *degree* of separation of ownership from control to the *impact* of this separation on the firm's performance. Morck, Shleifer, and Vishny (1986) examined the relationship between a company's performance and the number of shares held by the board of directors (owners). The authors argued that managers may become so "entrenched" through stock ownership that they may start to concentrate on their own utility rather than maximizing the firm's value. Recent investigations have centered on the *motives* and *effects* of varying ownership structures. Demsetz and Lehn (1985) argue that ownership structure is the result of firm characteristics rather than the cause for those characteristics. Using regression analysis on 511 of the largest firms in the United States, they found that corporate ownership is related to firm size, earnings and stock price variability, government regulations, and industry specificity.

Control of the agency problem in the decision-making process, then, is important when decision makers are not the major owners of the corporation. In such a situation, managers bear only a small part of the wealth effects of their actions and may be more likely to take actions that are not in the best interest of the stockholders. When decision management and control are concentrated in a small group of people, it would be fairly easy to engage in nonoptimizing behavior (from the stockholders' perspective.) The separation of decision management from decision control puts a set of checks and balances in the decision mechanism of the firm that makes is more difficult for the managers to undertake nonoptimal actions. In a corporation, the stockholders delegate the decision control function to the board of directors, who, in turn, delegate decision management and some decision control authority to the officers of the corporation.

To maximize their welfare, the shareholders of the firm wish to choose the proportion of the firm's shares owned by the managers that maximizes the value of their equity. An implicit assumption in shareholders' consideration is the impact of share ownership on the level of effort exercised by managers. Campbell and Kracaw (1985) argue that using share ownership can reduce the agency problem of shirking; however, share ownership by managers creates another agency problem, which is managers' incentive to choose investments that add to their benefits rather than investments that contribute to shareholders' wealth.

The impact of ownership structure and control on corporate productivity and efficiency was examined by a number of researchers. Some authors have concluded that the distribution of ownership has important implications for the efficiency and strategic development of the firm (Morris 1964; Williamson 1964; Galbraith 1967; Pfeffer & Salancik, 1978). Others have maintained that the distribution of ownership is insignificant (Jensen & Meckling 1976; Fama 1983; Demsetz 1983; Demsetz & Lehn 1985). Cubbin and Leech (1983) argue that research on this issue has yielded conflicting results because of problems with data and methods the researchers utilized in their attempt to construct meaningful measures of the distribution of ownership. Hill and Snell (1989), drawing on uniquely rich data on stock ownership published one time only by Corporate Data Exchange and measuring efficiency by productivity rather than profitability, found a positive relationship between stock concentration and productivity.

AGENCY, INFORMATION, AND MONITORING

A major objective of this book is to explain why different organizations entail different levels of control and information, and consequently, different levels of investments in information technology. In addition, the question of why we observe the control structure that we do will be addressed and dealt with. Pratt and Zeckhauser (1985) argue that in many circumstances where information does not flow freely, quite a few moderating devices are actually available (p. 5).

The root of agency theory is information economics. As a matter of fact, the economic building blocks of agency theory are information and incentives. In agency theory, people are assumed to be rational, maximizing individuals who do not have the same information in that either action or knowledge can be hidden. An agency relation is established when a principal(s) delegates the operation of his or her business to an agent(s). In the simplest agency model, when agents do not share information with principals, this will lead to inefficient risk bearing and/or inefficient effort choice. The principal may reduce this loss of welfare resulting from asymmetric information by requiring the more informed agent to report his or her private information. Agency research on this asymmetric information has demonstrated that a contract, which depends upon the information reported, leads to both (1) improved risk-sharing (See Christensen 1982; Baiman & Evans 1983; Peno 1984) and (2) improved effort choice (Melumad & Reichelstein 1986) over a contract without such information.

Managers with private information may be able to use this information to shirk, possibly making the principal worse off. Information may be public or private depending on whether the shareholders can observe it. Information is publicly observed if managers and shareholders can observe the signal from an informational system, and it is privately observed if only managers can observe the signal from an informational system. In addition, the relationship between managers and shareholders differs in the degree of informational asymmetry they entail. At one end of the spectrum, we have situations where the managers are fully controlled, and information flows freely and is fully shared with shareholders and the public. At the other end are positions in which managers have full discretion and are not observed at all by the shareholders. The perfect form of the latter scenario is seldom observed in the real world because shareholders could not totally trust managers unless their interests coincided (Pratt & Zeckhauser 1985).

Heckerman (1975) examined the impact of asymmetric information between managers and shareholders on investment decisions. He showed that there is an optimal wage that causes the manager to undertake only the projects the owner would like to finance and to reject all others. This settlement of the information asymmetry problem, however, hinges on substantial knowledge of the managers' preferences and qualities of the investment proposals available. Myers and Majluf (1984) and Miller and Rock (1985) showed that information asymmetries can cause some profitable investments to be rejected.

In related research, Diamond and Verrecchia (1982) show that information that is not used directly in a manager's contract may be utilized in an indirect way. The authors assume that a variable observable to both managers and shareholders must be the basis for the contract between the two parties. Further, information that can be observed by the shareholders and is expensive to communicate to managers should be an integral component of the managers' contracts. In an efficient market, shareholders, under such circumstances, will be able to trade the shares of the firm at prices reflecting this information.

Pratt and Zeckhauser (1985) argue that under a variety of conditions where information does not flow freely, a number of monitoring devices are, in fact, available. They also maintain that (1) shareholders would get less monitoring or monitoring of poor quality when monitoring is costly; (2) agency cost is extremely high when the interests of shareholders and managers conflict significantly, and information monitoring is expensive; (3) gains resulting from reducing agency cost are shared by both shareholders and managers; and (4) shareholders and managers have a common interest in identifying a monitoring structure that yields results as close as possible to ones that would result if information monitoring were costless. Shareholders desire information because it helps them to maximize their welfare. On the other hand, managers should be willing to share information because "information does not require exclusivity in use" (Allen 1990: 270).

THE BOARD OF DIRECTORS AS AN INFORMATION SYSTEM

The board of directors is the highest ranking body in a corporation whose members are elected by the shareholders of the firm. The board usually consists of members of the corporation (managers and officers) and nonmembers (outsiders). A large number of outside directors are senior managers of other corporations. The senior managers of the corporation who are represented on the board are expected to provide detailed knowledge of the firm's operations and activities (inside information). The role of outside directors is to improve the board's mechanism in monitoring managers.

Agency theorists view the board of directors as a mechanism for reducing agency cost arising from the problem of separation of ownership (risk bearing) and control (management) in a corporation. Since most corporations in the United States are run by a team of executives who own a small fraction of the firm's stock, management does not completely bear the negative consequences of any "non-value-maximizing behavior in which it engages" (Fosberg 1989: 26).

Several mechanisms have been recommended as a means of controlling this non-value-maximizing behavior of management; the board of directors is one of these mechanisms. Fama and Jensen (1983) argue that the board of directors is a particularly relevant informational system for controlling top executives and monitoring their behavior. From an agency perspective, then, boards can be used as monitoring devices for shareholders' interests. The important point to stress here is that when boards provide richer information, compensation of managers will be less likely to be based on a firm's performance. Rather, compensation will be more likely based on knowledge of executive behaviors because their behaviors are better known. In addition, when boards provide richer information, top executives are more likely to engage in behaviors that are consistent with stockholders' interests.[1]

By acting as an information system to stockholders, the board is satisfying its chief responsibility of managing the corporation and protecting the interests of the stockholders. At this level, management may be involved primarily in the formulation of policies and the evaluation of the performance of the officers. Specific tasks of the board members include declaring dividends, setting the salaries of officers, reviewing the system of internal control, authorizing officers to arrange loans from banks, and authorizing important contracts of various kinds.

The degree of participation in management by the board of directors varies from one company to another. In recent years, however, increasing importance has been attached to the inclusion on the boards of large corporations of individuals who were not officers of the companies and who could thus have a view independent of that of corporate officers.

Agency theory, which is rooted in economics and finance, is among the most recognized research on the role and contribution of the board of directors. Agency theorists argue that because of dispersion of corporate ownership, officers and managers of the corporation (agents) possess significant power. Without monitoring and control, these executives are believed to pursue objectives that may contradict those of the owners (principals); hence, shareholders' wealth maximization may be overlooked (Masson, 1971). Within this framework, the board of directors performs the function of monitoring and rewarding top-level executives to ensure the maximization of shareholders' wealth. In other words, the board of directors is considered to be the ultimate mechanism of corporate control (Zahra & Pearce 1989: 301).

From an agency perspective, the board enhances organizational performance by reducing agency costs arising from noncompliance of executives with established objectives and procedures; by emphasizing shareholders' objectives and focusing the attention of key executives on company performance; and through strategic decision making and control (Mizruchi 1983).

It is important to recognize that agency theory places a heavy weight on the board of directors' role as an arm for strategic control, especially the setting of guidelines for implementation of effective control measures. It is with this duty that sophisticated information technology is utilized. Although existing literature does not fully define the content of the board's role in strategic control, advocates believe that it becomes obvious at those critical points when important decisions must be made.

In addition to control, two other board tasks are postulated by agency theorists. These are service and strategy. The internal control role, however, is the most important of the three roles. In assessing the role of the board as a vehicle of corporate control, scholars tend to focus on executive compensation decisions. Compensation decisions are thought to reveal a board's evaluation of managerial competence and the CEO's contribution to the overall goal of increasing shareholders' wealth.

Although the agency view stresses the importance of the board's role as a strategic control element, few researchers have addressed this characteristic. According to Hector (1988), as the battles for corporate control continue to rise, it is believed that more researchers will look to the agency perspective as a suitable framework.[2]

Recently, increased litigation from shareholders and consumer activists has focused attention on the role of the boards of directors and the fulfillment of their responsibilities. Historically, directors have been held accountable only to shareholders. However, various factors are shaping a contemporary stance that holds that directors' primary responsibility is to the shareholders but recognizes that directors must give appropriate weight to the claims of other interested constituents of the firm (DuPlessis & Trenholm: 1991). To fulfill those added responsibilities, directors must possess more timely and accurate information, and this strengthens the case for more investments in information technology.

The role of the board of directors along with its responsibilities are being reshaped globally. In the 1989-1990 Price Waterhouse review of information technology and British policies computing investment, it was found that 503 organizations from the public and private sectors planned to increase their 1989 IT investment by 9 percent (Harvey 1989).

In the early 1980s, the Gillette company contracted with a firm for a custom version of a generic risk management program that was still under development. When the vendor shut down unexpectedly, Gillette was left in the cold. The risk management department at Gillette then decided to develop a system in-house. One of the main advantages to this system is that it has reduced the time needed to prepare the annual risk management report to Gillette's board of directors (McIntyre 1988).

As stated repeatedly, the organization's board of directors serves to ensure effective, competent corporate planning and decision making. In addition, a crucial task for any board is to determine its information use and need environments. Directors should periodically assess the quality and adequacy of the information they receive, and play an active role in ensuring that they get what they need. A properly designed set of information technology hardware and software systems helps corporate directors acquire the knowledge needed to fulfill their legal responsibilities. The minimum information requirements of such systems include: (1) background data, including all correspondence directed to the board, briefings on departmental activities, and the investment industry's analysis of the firm, (2) performance data, including monthly comparative financial statements, a monthly report of activities, audit and examination reports, and a monthly litigation report, and (3) planning data, such as acquisitions requiring board approval, annual projection of business expansion or retrenchment needs, and the organizations' goals and objectives (Alsup 1987).

The widespread acceptance of information technology, not only by

U.S. corporations but by foreign corporations as well, is evidenced through the direct use of this technology by management and board members. At many major companies in the United Kingdom, for instance, boards of directors are obtaining hardware from multidisciplined "information architects" who also are concerned with the board's wider needs. By using generalized software that incorporates a multidimensional data structure and various levels of information reporting, information architects offer systems that can be adapted quickly to an organization's specific needs. The benefits realized by a board of directors from this type of tactical control system include, but are not limited to: (1) graphical presentations, (2) automatic information capabilities, (3) increased speed of response, (4) accessibility, and (5) flexibility. It can be shown that the cost of providing this information with the use of informational technology is much less than the cost of providing it manually (Shoebridge 1986).

Cash et al. (1988) view the participation of information technology in an organization as being similar to the role of the board of directors. Viewing the IT role in this way, the authors believe that the key task of top-level management is to ensure that the board of directors will provide overall guidance to the IT department from its various interested constituencies.

SUMMARY

This chapter has been a review of the literature on agency theory and its relation to information, management ownership structure, and control, as well as a review of the board of directors as a control agent in the corporation. Although several studies have been undertaken to show how stock ownership by managers can reduce agency costs, until now there has been no attempt to study the interrelationship among control of the corporation, information and information technology, and management ownership structure from an agency point of view. The review of the literature on agency cost and management ownership structure covers the most empirical contributions since the mid-1970s. Some authors have argued that the distribution of ownership is a determinant of efficiency and strategic development of firms; others contend that the distribution of ownership struture is unrelated to performance or strategic development. The agency issue has been addressed by researchers in several disciplines. Some of these empirical studies have explained various phenomena from an agency perspective, including mergers and diversification, managerial resistance to takeover, representative versus corporate sales force, salary versus commission, type of transfer price, share price, acquisitions and divestitures, payment of greenmail, cost of equity, and golden parachute contracts.

The research on the separation of ownership and control developed gradually, and the focus soon shifted from the *degree* of separation of ownership from control to the *impact* of this separation on firm's performance. Further, recent investigations have centered on the *motives* and *effects* of varying ownership structures. Overall, empirical research has reached far less than satisfactory conclusions on this matter.

The coverage of the chapter was broadened to include the relationship between agency and information. The root of agency theory is in information economics. Studies in this respect examined the impact of asymmetric information between managers and shareholders on investment decisions, and concluded that there is an optimal wage that causes the manager to undertake only the projects the owner would like to finance and to reject all others. This settlement of the information asymmetry problem, however, hinges on substantial knowledge of the managers' preferences and qualities of the investment proposals available. Other studies showed that information asymmetries can cause some profitable investments to be rejected. Still other research showed that information that is not used directly in a manager's contract may be utilized in an indirect way.

The last section of this chapter covered the board of directors as a mechanism for reducing agency cost arising from the problem of separation of ownership (risk bearing) and control (management) in a corporation. It is argued that the board of directors is a particularly relevant informational system for controlling top executives and monitoting their behavior. From an agency perspective, then, boards can be used as monitoring devices for shareholders' interests. In addition to being a control agent, agency theorists argue that the board has two other tasks: service and strategy. This section concluded that little coverage has been provided in the literature for the strategic control element of the board of directors.

NOTES

1. For a useful review of agency theory and its applications, refer to Eizenhardt (1989) "Agency Theory: An Assessment and Review," *Academy of Management Journal*, Vol. 14, No.1, 57-74.

2. For an excellent review of the different perspectives on the role of the board of directors, refer to Zahra and Pearce "Boards of Directors and Corporate Financial Performance: A Review and Integrative Model," *Journal of Management*, 1989, Vol. 15, No. 2, 291-334.

4

The Management of
Information Technology

The terminology "information manager" emerged in the information systems literature several years ago. When it first surfaced, the job description of the information manager was vague and indistinct. However, it did not take long before a number of large companies promoted the information manager to a top management position and assigned him or her a new title, chief information officer (CIO). With the birth of the chief information officer, job descriptions and responsibilities started to, somehow, crystalize.

The CIO is a top management executive position with the responsibility for managing information and information technology's critical corporate resources from a global company-wide perspective. The creation of the chief information officer (CIO) position is one way to manage information and information technology investments better. As companies invest heavily in technology-based systems, they are vesting more control in technology strategists and CIOs, and many of these CIOs have invested much energy transforming their function from a service provider to a strategic partner with the business.

Since the CIO phenomenon is a relatively new one, many definitions of the term exist. Synnot and Gruber were among the first to offer a definition for the CIO. According to the two authors, a CIO is a senior executive responsible for establishing corporate information policy, standards and, management control over all corporate information resource. Ephraim McLean, associate professor of business at UCLA, defines the CIO as "the senior executive with primary responsibility for determining or advising the corporation on the flow or management of information" (Buday 1987: 23). Borbely (1985) states that a CIO is defined by the overall authority for policy, technology, and performance standards related to information resource management and applications, as well as for the development and management of interdepartmental or corporate systems and resources. Weiner and Girven (1985) maintain that a CIO is a generic title for an enterprise-level executive who takes part on a equal basis with other corporate officers in drawing the strategic path for the organization.

These different definitions of the chief information officer indicate the complexity in identifying the functions that distinguish that position from other positions in the organization. However, all of the above-stated definitions maintain that a CIO should (1) have a senior management presence and (2) be responsible for the management of informational resources at the corporate level. Only Weiner and Girven speak of the responsibility of the CIO in formulating the strategic course of the organization.

Many corporations have been using information technology to (1) draw the strategic path of the corporation, (2) create competitive opportunities both at the corporate and business levels, and (3) enhance more enduring connection between corporate strategic roles and IT investments. In general, many organizations have accepted the concept that IT can play a strategic role by creating competitive advantage rather than simply displacing costs. On the business level, and to realize a competitive position, those corporations have been using information technology in a variety of ways, such as the creation of interorganizational systems that connect customers, suppliers, and competitors to the organization's computers, and origination of systems supporting strategic decisions such as marketing analyses, cost management, control, and so on. Because the strategic information technology function has been evolving rapidly, it has affected its own structure and position within the corporation. Furthermore, the change in the view of information and information technology has been accompanied by a change in the role of information managers. It is believed that, in order to maintain a perspective on behalf of the whole organization, the structure responsible for information technology applications has to have a senior management presence and bring together the needs of end-user departments and the services of information technology providers. Even though the information technology department is still, in many companies, one of the ill-managed departments, the evolution of a new breed of senior-level managers, CIOs, is an indication of the endorsement by corporate executives of information technology as a vital strategic tool.

Promoting IT managers to corporate or executive positions reporting to the CEO or the CFO reflects a recognition of the strategic value of information technology to the organization. No matter how else the company attempts to support the matching process between information and information technology, on the one hand, and building competitive advantage, on the other, the top IT executive must be included in the "inner circle" of senior management for two critical reasons: (1) to communicate the strategic potential and limitations of information technology to senior management, and (2) to avoid the filtering of senior management business objectives through several layers before reaching the IT department (Guimaraes, Farrell, & Song 1988). In other words, the time and effort spent in officer meetings to discover the common ground between the IT officer and the business officers puts the company on firmer ground when it comes to making strategic IT investments that truly reflect business priorities.

According to Sprague and McNurlin (1986), four trends have set the parameters for defining the job of the chief information officer. The four core trends are hardware, software, data, and communications. One major trend has been the movement of hardware and processing power out of the control of the information systems department and into users departments. The software trends include "more discipline and rigor for in-house programmers, viable alternatives for *buy* rather than *make*, and increased involvement of users through prototyping or direct use of end-user software" (Sprague & McNurlin 1986: 26). The third core trend deals with allowing workers and managers in the organization to have direct access to data and information; this is what drove the trend toward distributed data bases. The fourth and final trend has to do with the advancement of communications equipment. Development of networks has increased interest in social and political issues, such as protecting the privacy of personal data, transborder data flows, and global data processing. These four trends have motivated executive officers and board members to create a top job for information manager.

The CIO's responsibilities are continuing to evolve. In recent years, information technology executives have become more and more concerned with organizational issues, such as communications with management and users, absorption of technology by the corporation, and the ability of information technology to respond quickly to changes in the inner and outer environments. In other words, the concerns of the CIO seem to be moving beyond technology toward the impact on the people, processes, and products of the corporation (Passino & Severance 1988).

The fever of the CIO phenomenon has been catching on rapidly in corporate America. In 1984, a Diebold survey of 130 major corporations found that one-third had someone in the CIO function, up from 5 percent of the same corporations in 1979 (Synnott 1987). In a 1989 *Computerworld* survey of 103 CEOs and other top business leaders in the Fortune 1000, 85 percent agreed that IT would hold the key to competitive advantage for their organizations in the 1990s; 88 percent said they believed information technology would significantly change the way their companies would do business in the 1990s (*Computerworld* April 1989).

The remainder of this chapter is organized as follows. The following section presents the set of hypotheses to be tested in the research. Then, the methodology and methods utilized in the research, including both univariate and multivariate methods, will be covered. This is to be followed by the results of the statistical tests. The chapter ends with some concluding remarks.

THE DEVELOPMENT OF HYPOTHESES

The set of hypotheses address the situation that arises when the individuals who control corporate resources do not own those resources. Managers may have a propensity toward perquisite, shirking, and non-value-maximizing behavior, and dispersion of stock ownership becomes a determining factor of who controls the corporation. As the shares become more and more widely held, and there is no longer a dominant stockholder, corporate management has greater leeway in decision making without a stockholder with sufficient shares (risk) to make management monitoring practical. In this situation, stockholders will push management to disclose information about the operations of the corporation.

As discussed in Chapter 3 of this book, agency theory highlights the importance of incentives and self-interest in organizational thinking. It suggests that much of organizational life is based on self-interest. Information is regarded as a commodity, in agency literature; it has a cost, and it can be purchased. This gives an important role to both formal and informal informational systems in an organizational setting.

Ownership structure of the corporation was investigated by Jensen and Meckling in 1976. The two authors maintained that equity ownership by managers would align their interests with those of the owners. As managers' equity increases, they tend to exercise tighter managerial control over the operations of their corporations and tend to demand more accurate information about the various operations of their companies. To accomplish that, those managers tend to be close to the day-to-day operations of their companies and to have more direct access to information needed in making their decisions. Further, managers with a high percentage of stock ownership tend to hire a CIO who reports to the CEO or the CFO, in most instances. Those managers would be willing to invest more in information technology, both hardware and software. In addition, since those managers place a high priority on getting the needed information in a timely manner, they believe that the creation of an information management position on the top management team is a priority. This in turn leads us to postulate that managers who have substantial equity positions within their firms (outcome-based contracts) are more likely to invest in information technology and to appoint a CIO on the top-level executive management team. As a consequence, the first hypothesis is formulated:

H01a: Equity ownership by managers is positively related to the creation of a CIO position on the top level management team.

Another particularly relevant informational control system for monitoring executive behavior is the board of directors. From an agency perspective, boards can be used as monitoring devices for shareholders' interests (Fama & Jensen 1983). Kosnik (1987) examined the board of directors as an informational mechanism for managerial opportunism. She studied 110 large U.S. corporations that were greenmail targets between 1979 and 1983. Using both hegemony and agency theories, she related board characteristics to whether greenmail was actually paid.

According to agency theory, the primary role of boards is to monitor actions of agents (executives) to ensure their efficiency and to protect principals' (owners') interests. Within this context, boards perform the critical function of monitoring and rewarding top executives to ensure maximization of shareholders' wealth. In essence, the board is seen as the ultimate mechanism of corporate control (Zahra & Pearce 1989). Following this approach, board contribution to organizational performance occurs by reducing agency cost arising from noncompliance of executives with established goals and procedures, by articulating shareholders' objectives and focusing the attention of key executives on company performance, and through strategic decision making and control (Mizruchi 1983).

The importance of board composition is prominently recognized in agency theory. Composition of the board reflects the extent to which management dominates the board. This is often judged by the ratio of outside to inside directors. The appointment of outside directors is important in achieving their responsibility in overseeing the performance of the CEO and salaried management teams. Outside directors may be better representatives of the traditional interests of stockholders by monitoring the overall effectiveness of management rather than giving routine approval of management programs. Outside directors, then, are considered essential for ensuring an effective system of checks and balances in a corporation. In addition, this ratio may be an important indicator of board independence in making decisions. Today, it is common to form an audit committee with several outside directors to ensure that the board will be objective in judging management performance.

Traditionally, then, directors have functioned as guardians of the financial interests of stockholders, with a specific concern for earnings and dividends. With time, responsibilities of the board of directors have increased, and recognition of the growing responsibilities is not entirely voluntary. On the one hand, the courts and the Securities and Exchange Commission (SEC) are actively involved in expanding areas of board responsibilities. In holding board members responsible, the SEC has taken a position that anyone in a position to know what is going on and to do something about it will be held liable. On the other hand, market dynamics have been very instrumental in disciplining outside directors for their services by pricing them according to their performances. The board, then, is perceived as an agent of control, and the more efficient, accurate, and timely information it has, the better it is for board members to make sound, rational, and informed decisions. Consequently, as the ratio of outside directors increases, CEO domination of the board becomes more difficult and directors are in a better position to exercise more control, that is managers will be squeezed for more timely and accurate information.

It is argued here that as the ratio of outside to inside directors increases, the need for better and more sophisticated informational systems will increase; hence, so will the need for a more specialized information technology manager to manage informational resources.

The reason for that is twofold. First, since there is a high number of outside directors not involved in the internal and routine operations of the firm, these have to be informed in a timely fashion to assist them in making rational, informed decisions, hence the need for an informational agent--the CIO--on the top management team along with more sophisticated IT equipment. The second reason is that inside directors who are mainly officers of the company would benefit from the presence of such an informational agent, who would be regarded by them as an "assurance factor" in dealing with outside board members. Based on the foregoing discussion, the second hypothesis is postulated:

H02a: There exists a positive relationship between the creation of a CIO position on the top management executive team and the ratio of outside to inside directors on the board.

In recent years, boards of directors have received stinging criticism that reflects a common theme. According to this view, for every instance of managerial abuse, there is a board of directors that--either by commission or omission--has endorsed or allowed such activity (Dalton & Kesner 1987). It has been further suggested that much of the board's inability to perform adequately in its role to control company management is related to its lack of independence from the very management it is unchartered to control (e.g., Kesner & Dalton 1986; Mintzberg 1983; Securities and Exchange Commission 1980). In addition, it has been argued that this tendency not to intervene when company management behaves in a manner inconsistent with the interests of the shareholders may be related to CEO duality (Dalton & Kesner 1987).

A very real threat to the exercise of independent judgment by the board of directors, and hence the erosion of its control function, is the dual role of the CEO as a board chairperson. Here, the top managerial officer of the corporation simultaneously serves as a chairperson of the board, which has the charter of monitoring and evaluating top management. Some scholars argue that this dual role suggests a certain conflict of interest, yet others seem to support the CEO/chairperson dual role by suggesting that "CEOs must direct the affairs of the corporation, serve as a bridge between the board and corporate management, and, above all, not be subordinate to anyone. If the final responsibility for the conduct of the corporation rests with the CEO, then so must the authority" (Rechner & Dalton,

1989: 142). It should be noted that although the debate over CEO/chairperson roles has been rich in verbosity, there has been only one empirical research brought to bear on this question. In a 1989 paper, Rechner and Dalton examined the question of the effect of the duality issue on the interest of shareholders as measured by stockholders returns, comparing returns of companies with CEO duality with the returns of firms with independent roles. Their results were, to say the least, interesting: They found no statistically significant difference. Although the single explanatory variable used is simplistic, this study is a step in the right direction in unraveling the duality issue.

In this book, the duality question is examined from a control point of view. Management would have more control over the well-being of the corporation and the way it functions if the CEO would serve as the chairperson of the board. Under such circumstances, the CEO would need more accurate and credible information to defend his or her position before the board members, hence the necessity to invest more in information technology and to appoint a chief information officer on the top-level executive management team. From this perspective, the CIO is perceived to be some sort of a "security blanket" for the CEO in the case of disagreement between the latter as a representative of the management of the corporation and the board of directors. This gives rise the following hypothesis

H03a: There exits a positive relationship between CEO duality in the corporation and the creation of a CIO position on the top level management team.

One of the principal assumptions of agency theory is that the various parties are rational, economic individuals who act in their self-interest. A conflict will occur between agents and principals because of individual self-interest. Agents (managers), for instance, attempt to maximize their own interests at the expense of principals' (equity holders' and debt holders') interests. Consequently, "agency costs" are incurred. There are two important components of agency costs--the agency cost of equity and the agency cost of monitoring and bonding (Morris 1987). The agency cost of equity is the decline of a firm's value when managers do not pursue the interests of shareholders. The agency cost of monitoring and bonding managers is the cost of control devices, such as "accounting reports, the incorporation of restrictive covenants in debt contracts, the establishment of management bonus plans related to reported profits, *and the establishment of sophisticated information systems* [author's italics]" (Morris 1987: 49). With more and more investment in information technology, the need for a top-level executive to manage those investments would increase and, consequently, so would the necessity to create a CIO position on the top-level management team.

Information technology and its management are thought of as monitoring devices employed to decrease agency cost. The question that arises is: Why are managers willing to expend resources (spend a fairly respectable portion of their budgets on the acquisition and maintenance of information technology and pay a high salary for an executive CIO) in order to decrease agency cost? According to Fama (1980), the welfare of the individual in the firm (managers, shareholders, or bondholders) depends on the survival of the firm. Therefore, reducing conflict among the members of the firm might result in an increase in the welfare of some without a decrease in the welfare of any of the others. Managers of corporations recognize that "the managerial labor market uses the performance of the firm to determine each manager's outside opportunity wage" (Fama 1980: 293). Manne (1965), one of the authors in the property-rights literature, examined the market of corporate control. He acknowledges that, with diffuse security, ownership management and risk bearing are mutually separate functions, and that disciplining management is an 'entrepreneurial job' that in the first instance falls on the firm's organizers, for example, boards of directors.

Conflict between managers and shareholders tends to occur more often in firms of larger sizes. Since the ownership of larger firms is generally more diversified than that of relatively smaller firms, this raises the likelihood of more conflicts between managers and shareholders. In this situation, owners will push the managers for more timely, accurate, and reliable information about the firm's activities. Consequently, the need for better information systems increases, and the designation of a CIO as part of the top management team would be looked at favorably by both management and the various shareholders. To the shareholders, even though the CIO is a member of management, he or she is thought of as an agent who increases the credibility of other managers and increases shareholders' confidence in the information released. To summarize then, as the size of the company increases, more diversified ownership is expected; consequently, more conflicts will arise among principals and agents; this leads, in turn, to agents requesting more accurate, timely, and credible information, which leads to more investment in information technology and to the creation of a CIO position on the top-level executive management team. This is formulated in a hypothesis format as follows:

H04a: There exists a positive relationship between the size of the firm and the creation of a CIO position on the top level executive management team.

Capital-intensive production techniques carry with them a more advanced technological level, and hence the use of information systems or information technology for production, running, and operating the technology. The more capital-intensive the corporation, the more investment in information technology, and the more crucial the need for a CIO on the top-level management team. In general, the ratio of fixed assets to the number of employees is used to measure the degree of capital intensity. The lower the ratio of fixed assets to the number of employees, the lower the capital intensity of the firm and, consequently, the lesser the likelihood of creating a CIO position on the top-level executive management team.

Companies within certain industries may obtain a substantial portion of their fixed assets through leasing agreements. However, current standards promulgated by the FASB require presentation of fixed assets acquired with capital leases on the balance sheet. Consequently, such assets will be included in the computation of fixed assets. Based on the above discussion, the following hypothesis is formulated:

H05a: There exists a positive relationship between capital intensity and the creation of a CIO position on the top-level executive management team.

Finally, it is believed that the level of investment in information technology as well as the creation of a CIO position on the top-level management team are industry-specific. This is logical since companies in such industries as the aerospace industry are expected to invest more in information technology than those companies in the food or apparel industries. Consequently, the industry variable will included as a dummy variable in the statistical analysis. Further, in order to be able to conduct the univariate tests, companies will be grouped in one of two categories. The first category contains those companies that are in high-technology industries (such as aerospace, petrochemicals, etc.) and the second category contains all other companies that were not classified in the first category. Consequently, the following hypothesis is formulated:

H06a: There exists a positive relationship between the technological level of the industry and the creation of a CIO
position on the top-level executive management team.

OVERVIEW OF METHODOLOGY

An empirical examination is conducted to determine the significant
organizational variables useful in explaining the phenomenon of
creating a CIO position on the top-level executive management team
that is used as a proxy for management recognition of the importance
of information technology, on the one hand, and the level of
investment in information technology, on the other. Specifically, an
experiment is designed to test the six hypotheses formulated in the
previous section. A cross-sectional matched-pair design is used to
compare corporations that had a CIO on the top-level management
executive team in 1988 to *similar* corporations that did not have one
for the same year. In a matched-pair design, one sample point from
each different population (firms with CIO and firms without CIO)
will be selected and matched together as one pair. The function of
a matched-pair design is to control for factors in the samples that are
being matched and to limit the effect of such controlled factors. Data
needed to test the set of hypotheses dealing with the level of
investment in information technology were collected by means of a
questionnaire/survey of a number of Fortune 500 companies
administered by the author. Tests of the hypotheses pertaining to the
presence of a CIO position will be presented in the remainder of this
chapter, whereas hypotheses concerned with the level of IT investments will be deferred to Chapter 5. The reason for this partition is
that Chapter 5 is reserved for discussing the questionnaire administered to collect data on IT investments from primary sources.
In other words, the data base utilized to test the hypotheses dealing
with the level of IT investment is different from that used in testing
those hypotheses concerned with the management of IT, that is,
having a CIO to manage all IT resources operationally and strategically.

Experimental Design

As mentioned in the previous section, a matched-pair design will be adopted in this study. In a matched-pair design, based on the factors (control variables) to be matched, one sample from each different population will be selected and matched together as one pair. The function of a matched-pair design is to control the factor that is being matched and to limit the effect of such controlled factor. The Standard Industrial Classification (SIC) is a statistical classification standard underlying all establishment-based federal economic statistics classified by industry. The SIC is used to promote the comparability of establishment data describing various facets of the U.S. economy. In order to control the substantive differences in the economic environment in different industries, the matched-pair factor is industry-specific. In other words, in order to minimize groupings in which firms have unrelated activities in an economic sense, the important point in the identification of similar firms will be the SIC (Baginski 1986: 202).

A cross-sectional experimental design is used to test the six hypotheses formulated previously. A cross-sectional experimental design is one type of correlational design, and is the simplest and most effective of the correlational designs in which all measurements are taken at one point in time. In other words, in empirical research, this design requires nothing more than the collection of two or more measures on a set of subjects or research entities at one point in time, and requires no treatments or manipulations. The cross-sectional approach is very useful in determining if two or more variables have any relationships and establishing those relationships. This design is very popular because of its ease, simplicity, and effectiveness. In this research, the relationships between the dependent variable (existence of a CIO) and independent variables (company-specific determinants of a CIO position) are examined. At the same time, the measures on the dependent variable and independent variables will be collected at signal time frame, for example, at a moment in time and not over time. This is necessitated by the fact that corporate information is issued at signal time frame and not over time.

The corporations in the experimental group were selected from the 1988 Fortune 500 industrial corporations that satisfied the following two criteria:

1. An examination of corporate officers of the corporation revealed the existence of a CIO position on the top level executive management team

2. The firm made the Fortune 500 list for three consecutive years (1986, 1987, and 1988).

This second criterion was deemed necessary to ensure that our sample was comprised of a set of *stable* Fortune 500 industrial corporations, and to safeguard against periodic fluctuations. Applying this criterion to the list of 1988 Fortune 500 firms resulted in 326 *stable* companies. Employing the first criterion on this *stable* set of companies resulted in a sample of 108 corporations. In other words, our experimental group of corporations with a CIO top management position consists of 108 corporations. Refer to Appendix I for a listing of companies in this experimental group.

The control group is composed of a set of 108 corporations from the population of 1988 Fortune 500 corporations that did not have a CIO on the top-level executive management team. The matching process of the experimental corporations was based upon the satisfaction of the following criteria:

1. The company made the list of Fortune 500 industrial corporations in the past three years; for example, the companies were selected from the *stable* set of the 326 companies identified above

2. Comparable primary industry based upon SIC codes, and

3. Comparable size based upon the 1988 revenues value.

These criteria were designed to identify the most compatible control subjects. For a list of companies comprising the control group (corporations without a CIO executive), refer to Appendix II.

Operational Measurements

In the current research, the determinants of hiring a CIO on the top-level executive management team is the dependent variable. The proposed measurements of the independent variables and dependent variable are presented below.

Independent Variables

Eight independent variables were identified based on the set of testable hypotheses presented above.

1. Management Ownership (MO). This variable will be measured by the ratio of the dollar value of company's stock held by top executives and managers of the company and the total value of the company's outstanding stock in 1988.

MO = value of stock owned by managers / value of
      company's stock

2. Firm Size. In our study, firm size is used as a proxy to measure agency cost. Information technology is thought of as a monitoring device employed to decrease agency cost. Since the ownership of larger firms is generally more diversified than that of relatively smaller firms, conflicts between managers and shareholders tend to occur more often in larger firms.

Previous research has used different measures for firm size. Notwithstanding the number of papers written on this subject, no cohesive or standard proxy variable to measure the variable size has emerged. To decrease the likelihood of using the wrong proxy, this research will employ three indicator variables to measure firm size: book value of gross assets (GA), total number of employees (EM), and total revenues (RE).

GA = book value of gross assets in millions of dollars
RE = revenues in millions of dollars
EM = number of employees in thousands.

3. Capital Intensity (CI). In general, the ratio of fixed assets to the number of employees is used to measure the degree of capital intensity. The lower the ratio of fixed assets to the number of employees, the lower the capital intensity of the firm, and, consequently, the higher the labor intensity. In this study, the ratio of gross fixed assets to the number of employees will be used to measure capital intensity. The purpose of using gross fixed assets is to avoid the problem of different depreciation methods used by firms in the same industry.

CI = gross fixed assets / number of employees

4. Ratio of Outside Board Members (OBD). Outside board members are those directors who are not employed by the company or retired from the company. The variable OBD will be measured by the ratio of the total number of outside directors to the total number of inside directors. Inside directors are those directors who are officers and managers or retired officers and managers of the company.

OBD = number of outsiders/number of insiders

5. Duality (DU). This is a binary variable that takes the value of one if the CEO of the company is also the chairperson of the board, and it takes the value zero if the chairperson of the board is different from the CEO.

DU = 1 for firms with a CEO/board chairperson dual role
DU = 0 for firms with different CEO and chairperson.

6. Industry Structure (IS). Companies in our experimental and control groups are classified into two categories based on the technological structure of their industries.

IS = 1 if firm is in a high-technology industry
IS = 0 if firm is not in a high-technology industry.

Dependent Variables

CIO = 1 for firms with a CIO
CIO = 0 for firms with no CIO
ITI = 1 for firms with a relative information advantage index[1] > 1
ITI = 0 for firms with a relative information advantage index < 1.

Table 4.1 summarizes the measurement of independent variables and the dependent variables.

Data Analysis and Functional Relationships

In this study, both univariate and multivariate analyses will be conducted. The purpose of univariate analysis is to identify any differences in characteristics between firms with a CIO and those without a CIO. For example, if the independent variable is company's book value of gross assets (GA), using univariate analysis

Table 4.1
Measures of Independent and Dependent Variables

Variables	Measures
CIO	= 1 for firms in the experimental group = 0 for firms in the control group
MO	The ratio of the dollar value of company stock held by top executives and managers of the company and the total value of company's outstanding stock
OBD	Ratio of outside to inside directors on the board; directors not employed by the company and not retired from the company
DU	= 1 for firms with a CEO/board chairperson dual role = 0 for firms with independent CEO and chair-person positions
GA	Gross fixed assets measured in millions of dollars
RE	Total revenues measured in millions of dollars
EM	Total number of employees measured in thousands
CI	The ratio of total fixed assets and total number of employees
IS	= 1 if firm is in a high-technology industry = 0 if firm is not in a high-technology industry

will help us understand whether there is any difference between the two groups of firms with respect to this variable. On the other hand, multivariate analysis is used to test the six hypotheses identified earlier in the chapter.

The functional relationships can be stated as follows:

$$CIO = f1\ (MO)$$
$$CIO = f2\ (GA)$$
$$CIO = f3\ (RE)$$
$$CIO = f4\ (EM)$$
$$CIO = f5\ (DU)$$
$$CIO = f6\ (OBD)$$
$$CIO = f7\ (CI)$$
$$CIO = f8\ (IS).$$

In the multivariate analysis, the functional relationship is determined as follows:

CIO = F (MO, GA, EM, DU, DU, OBD, CI, IS)

CHOICE OF STATISTICAL METHODS

Univariate Analysis

In the univariate analysis, the t-test statistic will be employed. As stated above, the purpose of univariate analysis is to distinguish characteristics between firms with CIOs and those without. The purpose of the t-test is to discriminate between two groups based on the characteristic of the independent variables. In other words, this statistical technique is a measure with which the independent variable discriminates between two groups of the dichotomous variable.

The t-test procedure computes a t-statistic for testing a hypothesis that the means of two groups of observations in a data set are equal. Means of the independent variables are computed for each of the two groups of observations, and then the t-test tests the hypothesis that the true means are the same. The underlying assumptions of the t-test procedure are that the variables are normally and independently distributed within each group. These two assumptions hold in our analysis, since the sample sizes are large enough to assure convergence normality.

The usual t-statistic for testing the equality of means Y1 and Y2 from two independent samples with n1 and n2 observations is:

$$t = (x1 - x2) / [s^2 (1 / n1) + (1 / n2)]$$

where s^2 is the pooled variance

$$s^2 = [(n1 - 1) s_1^2 + (n2 - 1) s_2^2] / (n1 + n2 - 2)$$

and where s_1^2 and s_2^2 are the sample variances of the two groups.

Multivariate Analysis

Special problems arise when the dependent variable is an indicator variable, as is the case in our analysis. Three problems are the most significant:

1. The error terms are nonnormal. For a binary 0, 1 dependent variable, each error term e = Y - (b0 + b1 X) can take only two values:

When Y = 1:   e = 1 - b0 - b1 x1
When Y = 0:   e = - b0 - b1 x1

Clearly, the normal error regression model, which assumes that the error terms are normally distributed, is not appropriate.

2. Error variances are nonconstant. Another problem with the error terms is that they do not have equal variances when the dependent variable is an indicator variable.

Hence, the error variances will differ at different levels of the independent variables, and the normality assumption is violated.

3. The response function is constrained. Since the response function represents probabilities when the dependent variable is a 0, 1 indicator variable, the mean responses should be constrained as follows:

$$0 = < E \{Y\} = < 1$$

Many response functions do not automatically possess this constraint. A linear response function, for instance, may fall outside the constraint limits within the range of the independent variable in the scope of the model.

The difficulties created by the this third problem are the most serious. One could use weighted least squares to handle the problem of unequal variances. In addition, with a large sample size, as is the case in our analysis, the method of least squares provides estimators that are asymptotically normal under quite general conditions, even if the distribution of the error terms is far from normal. However, the constraint on the mean response to be between 0 and 1 frequently will rule out linear regression models.

The use of linear regression analysis is inappropriate in our analysis, because in linear regression, the dependent variable is assumed to be continuous, which is not the case in our analysis; the dependent variable in this study is dichotomous and must equal either "0" or "1." When linear regression analysis is performed on qualitative dependent variables, it may seriously misstate the magnitude of the effects of independent variables, in that statistical inferences will not have any justification, and regression "estimates will at best approximate the true relationship only within the range of the data in the sample" (Aldrich & Nelson 1984: 28). Further, a study was conducted to determine how response group size and the number, distribution, and correlation of predictor variables affect empirical error rates and the minimum required sample size for using regression and logit analyses. Comparisons were made with error rates obtained from an ordinary least squares (OLS) linear probability model and the logit model. In addition, comparisons were made of the sensitivity of the logit and OLS parameter estimates to the range of data sampled for the predictor variables and the models' classificatory ability. Results of Monte Carlo simulations show that logit test statistics are biased when the sample size is small.

Discriminant analysis is also inappropriate to use in this study. When this type of research method is employed, the objective is to measure the characteristics of an individual or an object and, on the basis of these measurements, classify the individual or the object into one of two (or more) categories (Maddala 1983). Press and Wilson (1978) admit that although discriminant function estimators have been used instead of logit's maximum likelihood estimators, they have been found to be "generally inferior, although not always by a substantial amounts" (p. 699).

Both theoretical and empirical considerations, then, suggest that when the dependent variable is binary, the shape of the response function will frequently be curvilinear, which is shaped either as a tilted S or as a reverse tilted S, and that it is approximately linear except at the end. These response functions are called *logistic response functions*. They have asymptotes at 0 and 1, and then automatically meet the constraints on E{Y}. In the case of one explanatory variable, the functional format of the logistic function is:

$$E\{Y\} = [\exp (b0 + b1\,X)] / [1 + \exp (b0 + b1\,X)]$$

The logistic response functions are either monotonic increasing or monotonic decreasing, depending on the sign of b1. Further, they are almost linear in the range where E{Y} is between 0.2 and 0.8, and gradually approach 0 and 1 at the two ends of the X range. Another interesting property of logistic response functions is that they can easily be linearized

The logistic model is easily extended to more than one independent variable. As a matter of fact, "several independent variables are usually required with logistic regression to obtain adequate description and useful predictions" (Neter, Weasserman, & Kutner 1989: 595).

In the multivariate analysis, then, the logit regression analysis technique will be employed to test of the determinant variables. Logit regression analysis is a special model of multiple regression analysis. In classical regression analysis, all the dependent and independent variables are continuous. In the case of logit analysis, the dependent variable is discrete, and the independent variables are either discrete or continuous. In this book, because the CIO decision only appears in two different observable patterns (existence or nonexistence), logit regression analysis is the appropriate technique.

Logit regression analysis applies a logistic cumulative probability curve, which closely approximates a normal curve, except that the standard deviation of the standard logit function is 1.81 rather than 1 as in the normal distribution. The mean is 0, which is similar to the normal distribution. The logistic cumulative probability, p, is:

$$P\ (Y_i \mid X_i) = (1 + e^{-Y_i})^{-1} \quad i = 1, 2, ..., n$$

where Y_i is a linear function of the observable independent variables, X_is, and

$$Y_i = A + \Sigma B_i\ X_i$$
$$P\ (Y_i = 1 \mid X_i) = e^{Y_i} / (1 + e^{Y_i})$$
$$P\ (Y_i = 0 \mid X_i) = 1 - p(Y_i = 1 \mid X_i) = 1 / (1 + e^{Y_i}).$$

Applying the formula to our case

Y_i = 1 for companies with a CIO
Y_i = 0 for companies without CIO
X_is = determinants of a CIO position
$P\ (Y_i = 1 \mid X_i)$ = the probability of a company with a CIO
$P\ (Y_i = 0 \mid X_i)$ = the probability of a company without a CIO.

In order to estimate logit parameters, A and B_is, a method called Maximum Likelihood Estimation (MLE) is used. The purpose of MLE is to choose parameter estimates that imply the highest probability or likelihood of having obtained the observed sample Y_i (Aldrich & Nelson 1984: 51).

The maximum likelihood estimators of the parameters in the

logistic regression model are those values that maximize the logarithm of the likelihood function. To maximize the likelihood function, we take partial derivatives with respect to the parameters, set these equal to zero, replace the parameters with the estimators, and solve the resulting equations, called the *likelihood equations*, for the maximum likelihood estimators.

In logistic regression model building, independent variables and terms of interaction effects could be added or deleted in a direct manner. However, use of the all-possible-regressions approach is often restrictive because of the extensive numerical search calculations required to find the maximum likelihood estimates for a given logistic regression model. Consequently, stepwise selection procedures are frequently employed in logistic regression analysis.

The same types of inferences are of interest in logistic regression as for linear regression models. Two statistical inferences for logit analysis exist: first, individual coefficient estimates and, second, goodness-of-fit estimates. In individual coefficient estimates, the t-statistic is used to test whether an individual coefficient is significant. For the test of goodness-of-fit estimates, a Chi-square statistic is used. In other words, a Chi-square statistic is used to test the alternative hypothesis that all coefficients except the intercept are zeros.

A univariate dichotomous qualitative response model is constructed here using the independent variables identified above. The purpose is to examine the roles of those variables as determinants of a CIO position on the top level executive management team. Such models contain a qualitative dependent variable and an independent variable, and estimate to what extent each independent variable has an impact on the dependent variable and whether that impact is significant.

ESTIMATION RESULTS AND ANALYSIS

Publicly available data were collected on the operational variables described above for the 108 experimental and 108 control corporations. Because of limitation on data availability, 12 companies from the experimental group and four companies from the control group were excluded from the analysis. This, however, will in no way affect the viability of the statistical tests or the stability of the results, since the samples are large enough to be suitable representatives of the populations.

All data were collected from companies' proxy statements and annual reports. Where possible, these data were cross-validated from the proxies against information provided by the *Standard and Poor's Industrial Guide* and *Moody's Industrial Manual*.

Univariate statistics were developed for each group of corporations to determine if there were differences between firms that elect to have a CIO and those that elect not to have one. T-tests were computed to determine if the differences were statistically significant, and to measure the extent of the relationship between the dependent variable and each of the independent variables. Stock ownership by management and top executives of the company (MO) appears to be a determining factor in differentiating between the two group of firms: those with a CIO on the top-level executive management team and those without. As is shown in Table 4.2, the t-statistic is a significant -1.8822. This is statistically significant at the 90 percent confidence level.

The variable gross assets (GA) which, is used as one of the proxies for company's size, does not discriminate between companies with a CIO position and those without. In other words, size, as measured by the logarithm (Log) of gross assets, is not a determining factor in appointing a CIO on the top-level executive management team. The value of the t-statistic in Table 4.3 is -0.4962, which is not statistically significant.

The results of the t-test in Table 4.4 indicate that the variable revenues is not a discriminating variable between those companies with a CIO and those without one. The value of the t-statistic is 0.4203, which falls outside the boundaries of the 90 percent level interval of confidence.

Table 4.2.
Variable = MO

VP	N	Mean	Std Err	Min	Max
0	104	6.2477%	0.0081433	0.1%	44.5%
1	96	9.5780%	0.0161678	0.6%	99.5%

T	DF	Prob > T
-1.8822	198	0.0613

The number of employees of the company, which is used as one of the proxies for size, does not appear to be a determining attribute that discriminates between the two classes of firms, those with a CIO and those without. From Table 4.5, it is seen that the t-statistic is statistically insignificant at the 90 percent confidence level.

Table 4.3
Variable = LOG (GA)

VP	N	Mean	Std Err	Min	Max
0	105	7.6069	0.124145	5.3891	12.0080
1	96	7.6872	0.1010287	5.7557	10.9707
T		DF	Prob > T		
-0.4962		199	0.6203		

Table 4.4
Variable = LOG (RE)

VP	N	Mean	Std Err	Min	Max
0	105	7.7590	0.1096936	6.2186	11.7042
1	94	7.8766	0.0937031	6.2324	10.4763
T		DF	Prob > T		
-0.8075		199	0.4203		

Table 4.5
Variable = LOG (EM)

VP	N	Mean	Std Err	Min	Max
0	105	13.9690	0.1596994	19.2761	19.5464
1	94	14.1651	0.1419648	17.1507	344.56
T		DF	Prob > T		
-0.9115		199	0.3631		

The ratio of the number of outside to inside directors on the board appears to be a determining factor in differentiating between those companies with a CIO and those without. A t-statistic value of -3.227 falls well inside the 90 percent confidence interval (see Table 4.6). It is concluded, then, that the existence of a CIO is positively correlated with the number of outside directors on the board.

Table 4.7 shows that the number of directors on the board is not a significant attribute in differentiating between companies with a CIO and those without. The value of the t-statistic is -0.4219, which falls outside the boundaries of the 90 percent confidence interval.

As Table 4.8 shows, capital intensity is a significant variable in distinguishing between those firms with a CIO position on the top-level executive management team and those without. The t-statistic has a value of 1.7796 which falls well inside the boundaries of the 90 percent confidence interval.

As can be seen from Table 4.9, the duality of the company's CEO is not a determining characteristic in differentiating between companies with a CIO position and others without. The value of the t-

Table 4.6
Variable = OBD

VP	N	Mean	Std Err	Min	Max
0	104	3.1855	0.2065998	0.5714	13
1	94	4.4697	0.3506355	0.250	15
T		DF	Prob > T		
-3.2276		196	0.0015		

Table 4.7
Variable = BOD

VP	N	Mean	Std Err	MIN	Max
0	105	12.010	0.31593	5	22
1	96	12.219	0.41786	4	30
T		DF	Prob > T		
-0.4219		199	0.6735		

As can be seen from Table 4.9, the duality of the company's CEO is not a determining characteristic in differentiating between companies with a CIO position and others without. The value of the t-statistic is -1.4552, which is statistically insignificant at the 90 percent confidence level.

Table 4.8
Variable = CI

VP	N	Mean	Std Err	Min	Max
0	105	5.7112	0.46673	0.0062	2.2724
1	96	4.6263	0.38199	0.0180	18.6092
T		DF	Prob > T		
1.7796		199	0.0767		

Table 4.9
Variable = DU

VP	N	Mean	Std Err	Min	Max
0	104	0.7019	0.04507	0	1
1	96	0.7917	0.04167	0	1
T		DF	Prob > T		
-1.4552		198	0.1472		

Table 4.10
Variable = IS

VP	N	Mean	Std Err	Min	Max
0	105	0.3524	0.046844	0	1
1	96	0.6146	0.049934	0	1
T		DF	Prob > T		
-3.8296		199	0.0002		

Table 4.10 displays the results for testing the hypothesis that industry structure is not a determinant of a CIO position. This null hypothesis is not supported given a value of -3.8296 for the t-statistic, which is significant at the 99 percent level. It is concluded, then, that the technological level of the industry is a determining characteristic for appointing a CIO on the top-level executive management team.

It is important to note here that the results of the t-test regarding the proxies utilized to measure size (gross assets, revenues, and number of employees) do in fact increase the confidence in the representativeness of the two sample groups (experimental and control). Companies in the two groups were matched based on size, and it is no surprise to find size indicators to be statistically insignificant in differentiating between the two groups.

Univariate tests are important first steps in analyzing the data, but the multivariate tests help promote an understanding of the interactive effect of the combined independent variables on the dependent variable. Multivariate tests also help as a check on multicollinearity and other measurement problems (Chow 1982).

Logit analysis is used to determine the variables which have a significant impact upon the decision of appointing a CIO. Using maximum likelihood techniques, the logit model is estimated and, as a result, the test statistics of the model follow a Chi-square distribution. The logit transformation also constrains the probability estimates between 0 and 1. In addition, when used with a polychotomous dependent variable, no ordinal properties are assumed, only nominal.

The coefficient of determination (R^2) used in regression analysis to evaluate how well the independent variables explain the changes in the dependent variable is lacking in logit analysis. Instead, the validity of a particular model is based upon the classification accuracy of the model. For a set baseline (cutoff point), predictive accuracy is based on the percentage of the total number of correct classifications out of the total sample. A standard cutoff has been 0.5, meaning that probabilities under 50 percent are classified as $Y = 0$, and probabilities of 50 percent or greater are categorized as $Y = 1$.

Multivariate Results

The functional logistic regression equation was constructed as follows,

CIO = F (MO, GA, RE, EM, OBD, CI, DU, IS)

where CIO, MO, GA, RE, EM, OBD, CI, DU, and IS are the variables identified in the section headed Operational Measurements.

When testing a number of hypotheses simultaneously, a deficiency of independence between the hypotheses being investigated will emerge. Because of this, the significance levels presented in the research symbolize relative significance. In other words, the p-values resulting from the logit analysis are actually "understated" and can only be used to represent the relative significance of the variables tested. For example, if X1 has a lower p-value than X2, that indicates only that X1 has greater impact than X2. Therefore, it is important not to place too much confidence on the reported levels of significance.

The eight independent variables were analyzed using the MLE procedure which evaluates the relative importance of the eight control variables in predicting the likelihood that a company will have a CIO on its top-level executive management team. The results from the logistic regression analysis with the eight control variables are presented in Table 4.11. As can be seen, only three variables are statistically significant at the 95 percent confidence level. Those are industry structure (IS), management ownership (MO), and the ratio of inside to outside directors on the board (OBD). The other five variables were found to be insignificant. However, as mentioned above, a deficiency of independence among the hypotheses tested will emerge when these hypotheses are tested simultaneously. This leads us to use caution when interpreting the relevance of the p-values, which symbolize the statistical significance of the variables. Specifically, the p-values resulting from the logit analysis can only be used to represent the relative significance of the variables tested. In other words, it can be confidently stated that the ratio of outside to inside directors on the board has a stronger impact on the decision to appoint a CIO on the top-level executive management team than the magnitude of management stock ownership.

In logit analysis, there exists one assumption regarding the independent variables: They have to be uncorrelated with each other. In other words, no multicollinearity is detected. Multicollinearity among several independent variables is said to exist when a nearly exact linear relationship exists among these variables. Several ways exist to detect multicollinearity. In this book, The Pearson Correlation Coefficient is used to test the multicollinearity among independent variables. Table 4.12 represents the matrix of correlation coefficients among the eight independent variables used in the logistic regression for the whole model.

Table 4.11
Logit Results with All Variables

Variable	Beta	Std Err	Chi-Square	P
Intercept	3.24734	2.935585	1.22	0.2686
MO	2.72805	1.559507	3.06	0.0802
GA	-0.99262	0.672787	2.18	0.1401
RE	0.81706	0.624426	1.71	0.1907
EM	-0.17477	0.316634	0.30	0.5816
BD	0.14816	0.062935	5.54	0.0186
CI	-0.45748	1.428394	0.10	0.7488
DU	0.24252	0.376009	0.42	0.5189
IS	0.94955	0.324554	8.56	0.0034

As can be seen, the three indicators of size (GA, RE, and EM) are highly multicollinear with each other and with other variables in the model. Severe multicollinearity in logit regression leads to overestimation of the results. To correct for the problem of multicollinearity, several remedies exist, the best of which is to eliminate the variables that are highly multicollinear with each other.

The three highly multicollinear variables (GA, RE, and EM) were eliminated from the model, and a stepwise logit regression analysis was run on the remaining variables. Table 4.13 represents the results of the stepwise logit regression. This procedure selected three variables for inclusion in the model. The Chi-square value for the overall model was 26.82 with three degrees of freedom (significant at the 0.0001 level). In other words, the model as a whole is statistically significant as indicated by the p-value (0.0001). These results indicate that hypotheses H01a, H02a, and H06a are supported, with management ownership structure, industry structure, and board composition affecting the decision to create a CIO position on the top-level executive management team in a positive way. In other words, as the level of management ownership increases, the likelihood of appointing a CIO on the top-level executive management team will increase. In the same vein, as the number of outside directors on the board increases, so will the likelihood of hiring a CIO to manage IT resources. The size of the corporation (as measured by revenues, gross fixed assets, and number of employees), capital intensity, and duality of the CEO had no significant direct effect on a top executive CIO presence. In other word, hypotheses H03a, H04a, and H05a were not supported by the analysis.

Table 4.12
Correlation Matrix for the Nine Independent Variables

	MO	GA	RE	EM	OBD	CI	DU	IS
MO	1.0000	-0.1883	-0.1949	-0.1536	-0.0395	-0.0253	0.0030	-0.0292
	0.0000	0.0076	0.0057	0.0298	0.5799	0.7214	0.9657	0.3286
GA		1.0000	0.9457	0.7838	0.1195	0.2401	0.2691	0.1221
		0.0000	0.0001	0.0001	0.0935	0.0006	0.0001	0.0842
RE			1.0000	0.8545	0.1381	0.1043	0.2731	0.1712
			0.0000	0.0001	0.0524	0.1405	0.0001	0.0151
EM				1.0000	0.2008	-0.2870	0.2539	0.1336
				0.0000	0.0046	0.0001	0.0003	0.0586
OBD					1.0000	-0.0809	0.1509	0.0755
					0.0000	0.2572	0.0337	0.2903
CI						1.0000	0.0314	-0.0132
						0.0000	0.6588	0.8525
DU							1.0000	0.0339
							0.0000	0.6329
IS								1.0000
								0.0000

Table 4.13
Stepwise Logit Results

Variable	Beta	Std Err	Chi-Square	P
Intercept	-1.50063	0.340147	19.46	0.0001
IS	1.07486	0.309137	12.09	0.0005
OBD	0.17838	0.061184	8.50	0.0036
MO	2.93453	1.474787	3.96	0.0466

Notes:
N = 201.

Goodness of fit for the test: $G^2 = 247.17$. $G^2 = -2 \log (L_0 / L_1)$, where L_1 is the value of the likelihood function for the full model as fitted and L_0 is the maximum value of the likelihood function if all coefficients except the intercept are 0.

The three significant variables correctly classified 64.6 percent of the subjects with a type-I error of 37.5 percent and type-II error of 33.3 percent. Table 4.14 is a classification table that highlights the model's classification ability.

SUMMARY

The objective of this chapter was to identify those company-specific factors that affect the creation of a CIO position on the top-level executive management team to manage information and information technology in an organization. It is needless to utter the far-reaching impacts that advances in information and information technology have had on the internal structure and processes of the organization, especially the control function. Formal control systems employed by corporations include budgeting and boards of directors; managerial supervision is an informal control system. Information technology penetrates all formal and informal systems in addition to acting as a control system by itself. It is argued that as managerial supervision increases (more effective control), the need for well-managed informational systems increases, hence the necessity for a top-level

Table 4.14
Classification Ability of Model

		Predicted		
		Negative	Positive	Total
	Negative	68	36	104 (50%)
True				
	Positive	34	60	94 (50%)
		102 (48.5%)	96 (51.5%)	198 (100)

Sensitivity: 63.8%; Specificity: 65.4%; Correct: 64.6%;
False positive rate: 37.5%; False negative rate: 33.3%.

executive position to manage those informational systems and to act as a liaison between the various informational departments, on the one hand, and the CEO and other executives, on the other.

The statistical analysis identified a number of company-specific characteristics that are significantly related to the creation of a CIO top executive position where the CIO acts as an "informational control agent"; these characteristics were empirically identified as management equity ownership, industry structure, and the composition of the board of directors. The findings support the first hypothesis that when management equity ownership is high, managers would, naturally, be more involved in the close monitoring of the company's activities and the collection of information; hence, the need for an independent informational "agent" (CIO) increases. As was stated in the chapter, the role of the CIO in a top executive position is to provide a relatively low-cost mechanism for assuring the survival of the company and other members of the top management team, and decrease the likelihood of their replacement or reordering; this mechanism is less costly than the management disciplining mechanisms provided by market dynamics. Consequently, as the equity held by top management increases, their managerial supervision increases because of increased economic interest. In the absence of an informational "agent", this might lead to sacrificing managers' interests as stockholders. Empirically, a statistically significant positive relationship was found between the existence of a top-level executive CIO and the level of management stock ownership.

The finding that companies with a relatively large number of outside directors tend to have a CIO in an executive position supports the premise of agency theory that more outside board members means better attention to stockholders' interests. Also, in order for outside board members to better serve their constituents, they need to have access to more timely information. As a result, they will push for better management of information technology resources and, consequently, the creation of a CIO position on the top-level executive management team.

The study failed to support the hypothesis of agency cost as exemplified by the size of the corporation. According to the firm size hypothesis as postulated in this book, the larger the firm ,the greater the likelihood of hiring a CIO on the top management executive team. The implication of the empirical test did not support the firm size hypothesis. A possible explanation for this unexpected result is the choice of the experimental and control groups. As mentioned in the methodology section, the choice of the corporations was based on a matched-pair design, and the matching variable was size as measured by revenues. In other words, the impact, if any, of the size variable was neutralized through the sample selection process. Another possible reason is that the creation of a CIO position on the top-level management team might be related to the structure and complexity of the organization more than its size. The more complex the corporation, the more the need for a high-level informational integrator.

This research did not support the capital intensity hypothesis by finding a statistically insignificant association between the capital intensity of a corporation as measured by the ratio of fixed assets to the total number of employees and the presence of a CIO on the top-level executive management team. Since capital intensity (CI) was measured as the ratio of gross fixed assets (GA) and the number of employees (EM), its impact, if there is any, was also neutralized by the sample selection process.

This research has isolated three variables that aid in the explanation of the phenomenon of a CIO creation on the top-level executive management team. Two variables are related to the management of the company, management equity ownership and the composition of the board of directors; the third variable has to do with a structural component, the technological level of a corporation. The model correctly classified an approximate 65 percent of the companies in a sample of 108 matched-pair firms. Other variables were postulated to be strong candidates as potential determinants of a CIO top executive position, such as company size, which was used as a proxy for agency cost, and duality. These variables, however, were not selected by the logit analysis model.

NOTE

1. Refer to Chapter 5 of this book for a discussion of relative information technology index and its derivation.

5

An Empirical Analysis
of Information Technology

One of the most critical concerns in information technology (IT)-related research has been the conceptualization and measurement of this technology. Over the years, IT has been conceptualized and measured differently by the different researchers who undertook such an exercise. The majority of the authors, however, parallel information technology with computer systems. Whisler (1970), for instance, defines IT as the computer-based technology of sensing, coding, transmitting, translating, and transforming information. Robey (1977) describes IT as the installation of computer-based information systems. Recently, Cash, McFarlan, and McKinney (1983) defined information technology as the integration of telecommunications, data processing, and office automation. Buchanan and Boddy (1983) define information technology as all technology dealing with computer-aided manufacturing and computer-aided administration.

More recently, Weill and Olson (1989) provided a more precise definition of information technology by classifying it into three different categories: strategic, informational, and transactional. According to this author, the main reason for this classification is that "investments are generally made for different management objectives and thus they should be matched with appropriate performance measures" (p. 25). Strategic IT investments are those that change the company's product or the way the firm does business vis-a-vis its competitors. The main objective of strategic IT is to provide competitive advantage. Informational IT promotes management control and short-term planning, such as resource acquisition.

Finally, transactional IT helps managers at the operations level such as accounts payable and inventory management.

Over the past two decades, large global corporations have made enormous investments in IT. A comprehensive study conducted by The Diebold Group in 1984 found that, on the average, information technology expenditures accounted for 1.44 percent of total revenues. Further, research has revealed that investment levels varied significantly by industry. A study of small manufacturing firms (Delone 1988) revealed an average investment in IT of 1 percent of sales; in the service sector, however, IT investment comprised 15.5 percent of capital stock in 1985.[1] In the insurance industry, average investment in IT for 1986 was approximated at 2 percent of premium income (Harris & Katz 1988), whereas IT investment in the retailing industry was 3.2 percent of revenues (*Computerworld* 1987). A PIMS 1984 study found that the average IT expenditure was 30 percent of management costs (equivalent to 8 percent of total revenues) for top performing companies but averaged 2 percent of revenues for the whole sample of companies surveyed. This is another indication that some kind of relationship exists between the level of IT investments and revenues. Datamation budget survey indicates that, in 1987, approximately 0.6 percent of manufacturing firm revenues were invested in IT. These figures reflect only centralized management information systems (MIS) expenditures. The actual firm-wide expenditure on IT is remarkably higher as a result of spending by functional departments which is not included in these figures (Weill & Olson 1989).

This chapter is devoted to examining the relationship between information technology and performance. It is organized as follows: The following section reviews the literature dealing with the relationship between IT investment and a company's performance, both theoretically and empirically. Both the advantages and shortcomings of the different methodologies employed in these studies are covered. This is followed by a section dealing with the design of the questionnaire employed as a means to collect data from a sample of companies in the U.S. The development of a new indicator of IT performance, the relative IT index (ITI), is covered in the next section. The section that follows presents the results from both the univariate and multivariate analysis. The chapter closes with a concluding section.

IT INVESTMENT AND PERFORMANCE

A number of scholars have studied various aspects of IT investment and its impact on a company's performance. A number of those argue that the decision of how heavily to invest in IT is difficult and is integral to the overall decision as to the optimal mix of capital and labor employed by a firm. In addition, those studies have used a variety of means to measure the amounts of IT investments, on the one hand, and performance, on the other hand.

Leading studies in this area were those conducted by Lucas in 1975. The first study conducted by Lucas was on a sample of 165 branches of a California bank, where the utilization of information technology was emphasized as the key proxy variable rather than IT investment. In surveying the 165 branches of this bank, he found that the use of information technology did not account for a great proportion of the variance in a unit's performance. In a second study, however, Lucas found that in some industries there was a slight correlation between performance and the use of information technology.

The second important study conducted in this domain was that of Cron and Sobol (1983). The two authors carried out a comprehensive study using a sample of warehousing companies and employing three indicators of information technology:

* Computer ownership
* Number of standard application areas computerized
* Types of application areas computerized.

The findings of Cron and Sobol revealed that companies that make extensive use of computers and information technology are either very strong or very weak financial performers. The most important of their findings though was the promotion of the strategic literature, which underscores the importance of the strategic position of the company. In other words, Cron and Sobol's findings substantiate the view that if a company occupies a strong strategic position, more investment in information technology will improve its performance. On the other hand, if a firm is in a weak strategic position, IT investment will not be more than an added expense (Strassmann 1985).

In a study of 58 banks, and using the ratio of data processing expenditures to total assets and the number of functional areas with computerized applications as proxies of IT investment, Turner (1985) failed to find any relationship between organizational performance and the relative proportion of resources allocated to data processing.

Strassmann (1985) examined a number of top performing companies and compared them with a sample of average performing companies to determine whether any consistent differences in the investment in and applications of IT were observable. Despite the fact that his findings were not totally consistent, generally, market leaders have been shown to have invested more heavily in IT, as a percent of sales, than have the average performers.

Roache (1987) studied the service sector using data from the Department of Commerce. His indicator variable was the percent of capital stock utilized. The conclusion of his research indicates that heavy investment in information technology did not contribute to increasing productivity, in general, in the 1980s. The indicator variable used by Roache, however, has received a number of criticisms on the grounds that funds that are disbursed annually were not included in this measure.

In his 1986 study of the insurance industry, Bender found that there was an optimal level of investment in information technology. He broke IT investments down into several components and found that only expenditures on information systems people, hardware, and environment were significant. He also found a positive correlation between financial performance and investment in information processing. In addition, by plotting IT investment against organizational performance, as measured by total revenues, he showed that an optimal performance was reached at a range of investment in IT between 20 to 25 percent of total revenues.

In a 1987 paper, Weill conducted six mini case studies in five different industries. As a result of his study, a new concept was conceived in the area of IT investment and performance--conversion effectiveness. Conversion effectiveness is viewed by the author as the quality of organization-wide management and commitment to IT. Four elements of conversion effectiveness emerged form the six mini case studies; these are: (1) top management commitment to IT, (2) previous firm experience with IT, (3) user satisfaction with systems, and (4) the turbulence of the political environment of the organization. The relationship between performance and IT investment is believed to be moderated by the conversion effectiveness of the company. Companies that convert IT investment more effectively will have sounder relationships between IT investments and performance than those companies with low conversion effectiveness.

DeLone (1988) examined a sample of 93 small manufacturing firms in California. He found that IT investment averaged 1 percent of sales in this sample, and concluded that the key to the realization of the potential impact of IT investment was the degree of involvement of the chief executive officer (CEO).

Over a period of four years, Katz and Harris conducted research on 40 insurance companies. Their findings, which were published in a paper in 1988, revealed that the most profitable firms in the sample were more likely to spend a significantly higher proportion of their noninterest operating expenses on information technology. Causality was not established, however, leaving the door wide open to speculation as to whether IT investment causes performance or vice versa.

There are a number of reasons why these different studies reached conflicting or inconclusive results. First, the authors used different proxies to measure the level of IT investment. Lucas, for instance used the utilization of information technology as a proxy for IT investment, whereas Cron and Sobol utilized three measures: computer ownership, number of standard application areas computerized, and types of application areas. The use of different proxies would rationally lead to different conclusions. Second, the authors employed different indicators to measure performance. Although Harris and Katz employed premium income as a performance measure, total revenues were the performance measure in Bender's study. The use of different performance measures would lead to different results. Third, the authors conducted their empirical investigations on qualitatively different industries. These ranged from manufacturing to insurance, to banks, and so on. Given that different industries have different levels of competition, financial strengths, structure, regulations, and so forth, investment in information technology would affect their performance in dissimilar fashions. Last, the different authors employed varying methods to collect their data. Some utilized questionnaires, whereas others relied on personal interviews. Different research designs would yield different levels of data validity and reliability, which in turn would lead to different research conclusions.

The foregoing discussion suggests that the research on the relationship between information technology and performance is still in its infancy. There is a long and thorny road ahead for researchers and practitioners in this respect. Kathy Curley and John Henderson (1989) suggest that IT investment payoff be examined at four different levels. The first is the macroeconomic level, wherein gross economic aggregations may be employed to examine the impact of IT investment on the overall national economy. The major weakness of this level of analysis lies in the unreliability and uncertainty of the input data, on the one hand, and the multicollinearity of econometric variables used in the analysis. The second is the level of the firm, or strategic business units (SBU), where concerns center on competitiveness and business strategy. Most of the studies reviewed above were at the SBU level. Although they have a number of limitations and shortcomings, the findings of these studies have, in general, been more encouraging than the macroeconomic studies. The shortcomings of studies at the business level include small sample size, restricted variability and unproven causality (Huff 1990).

The third is the functional unit or the level of subgroups within an organization, departments, or project teams. On this front, there have been two major findings. The first is that the most significant impacts of IT introduced into work groups have not been those originally anticipated. The second key finding has been that intangible benefits have not been translated into benefits to the organization as a whole (Huff 1990). In other words, emphasis has been on the benefits of information technology and not on its value to the organization.

The fourth is the individual level. This is the most extensively studied to date. Much of the research on this level has been concerned with the impact of IT on task-specific issues, such as the improvements of efficiency of data entry clerks or word processing staff as a result of new IT investments.

An examination of the actual behavior of a number of organizations regarding the issue of IT investments and questions such as when to invest, where to invest, and how much to invest leads one to conclude that in the absence of a set of standard guidelines and well-defined IT policies, an organization can be driven back on its own resources. Information technology investments can be enhanced by the existence of a corporate policy that includes guidelines for major business activities that will require detailed procedures and standards to cover all IT issues. Approaches to planning a strategy for issuing such a policy must take into consideration: (1) organizational goals and objectives, (2) organizational attributes, and (3) agreement with established organizational policies. Support for developing such a policy should be given by the board of directors. In addition, organizational policies should include specific statements concerning such areas as organizational structure, performance, and funding.

INSTRUMENT DESIGN: THE QUESTIONNAIRE AND ITS TABULATION

Different types of research designs are appropriate to different questions and situations. Field research utilizing a well-designed questionnaire has been held to be the most appropriate when little is known about the area of interest or if the available data is spotty. Further, the likelihood of obtaining reliable and valid results when using this method is increased by the inclusion of the appropriate sample of firms in the study.

To collect data on the levels of IT investments, a questionnaire was designed and mailed to a sample of companies in the United States. The design of the questionnaire was carefully orchestrated. Questions were formulated based on a thorough review of the literature and past research. Basically, the questionnaire consisted of three separate sections and a total of 19 questions. A review of the literature suggested the types of questions and, consequently, the variables to be included in the questionnaire. It was constructed so that both quantitative and qualitative data would be relatively easy to collect and analyze. The questionnaire consisted of factual questions about pertinent factors, so that meaningful relationships between independent variables and dependent variable could be examined. To make the job of the respondent easier, only structured questions were included in the survey instrument. Although unstructured questions are useful in exploratory studies in which various dimensions and facets of the problem are examined (Busha & Harter 1980), it was deemed necessary to exclude them from this instrument in order to increase response rate. Since it is usually harder for respondents to answer unstructured questions, they will, in most instances, elect not to participate in the survey. The questionnaire was accompanied by a letter in which anonymity of the responding company was guaranteed. Approximately 90 percent of the respondents, however, provided their names and their titles.

Over a period of one year, the questionnaire was sent to 305 top information technology executives identified through *The Directory of Top Computer Executives* (1988). This directory provides the names and titles of individuals who head the information technology department in their respective organizations. The author received 64 responses of which 57 were complete and valid. This comprised an approximate 21 percent reply rate. In empirical analysis, this is a good reply rate. Table 5.1 is a summary of the distribution of respondent firms by industry.

Table 5.1
Sample Distribution by Industry

Industry	Number	Percentage
Aerospace	6	9.375%
Chemicals	9	14.062%
Computers	7	10.937%
Electronics	6	9.375%
Food	8	12.500%
Metals	2	3.125%
Petroleum Refining	6	9.375%
Pharmaceutical	9	14.062%
Publishing	3	4.687%
Scientific Equipments	7	10.937%
Soaps, Cosmetics	1	1.562%
TOTAL	64	100.00 %

As mentioned above, the questionnaire consisted of three sections. The first section included six questions formulated with the primary objective of gaining a clear and precise understanding of how heavily the firm is investing in information technology. Questions dealt with the value of hardware and software, as well as the number of personnel in IT-related jobs. Table 5.2 provides a descriptive industry classification of the sample of respondent companies.

The first question asked the respondent to provide the total value of IT assets, including hardware and software. As can be seen from Table 5.2, the maximum value of $1200 million was provided by a company in the aerospace industry, and the minimum value of $1.1 million was provided by a company in the chemical industry. The total book value of IT for the 57 respondent companies averaged $115.77 millions in 1988-1989 with a standard deviation of $208.70 millions.

The second question asked the respondent to furnish a value for the estimated annual IT budget. The maximum value of $950 million was provided by the same aerospace firm with maximum book value, and the minimum budget figure of $950 thousands was furnished by a chemical firm. The average figure for the 57 respondent firms was $147.89 millions with a standard deviation of $234.31 millions (see Table 5.2).

Table 5.2
Descriptive Statistical Summary of Section I of the Questionnaire

	Max	Min	Mean	Std Err
IT Asset Value	$1,200[1]	$0.95	$115.8	$208.7
Annual IT Budget	$ 950	$1.00	$147.9	$234.3
% of Budget Spent on Staff	66%	20%	41.5%	13.7%
Number of IT Staff	8,000	17	1,040	1,703
Number of Computers and Terminals	70,000	200	11,839	18,598

[1] Numbers are in millions of U.S. dollars

Question three dealt with the percentage of IT budget spent on personnel. This question was geared towards measuring the degree of automation on the firm level and the extent of staff involvement in managing information technology. As seen from Table 5.2, the maximum value in the sample of respondent companies was 66 percent, and it was provided by a firm in the chemical industry. The minimum value of 20 percent, on the other hand, was provided by three firms: a computer manufacturer, a firm in the chemical industry, and a firm in the food industry. The average figure for the 57 respondent firms in the sample was 41.46 percent with a standard deviation of 13.67 percent.

The fourth question considered the number of employees involved in information technology, both those in managerial and technical positions. The maximum figure in the sample of respondents was 8,000 employees. It is interesting to note that this figure was provided by the same aerospace firm that ranked at the top in terms of total IT assets and annual budget. The company that ranked second in terms of the number of IT employees was another firm from the aerospace industry with a total of 5,600 employees. The minimum figure provided was 17 employees. This was furnished by the same chemical company that placed at the bottom in terms of total IT assets. This leads us to believe that there is some degree of correlation among these indicator variables. The average figure for the whole sample is 1,040 employees with a standard deviation of 1,703 employees.

Question number five in this section explored the number of personal computers and terminals in the company. The maximum value of 70,000 units was provided by a firm in the aerospace industry and the minimum value of 200 was furnished by a firm in the food industry. The number of personal computers and terminals averaged 11,839 computers and terminals for the sample of 57 respondent companies with a standard deviation of 18,598 (see Table 5.2).

The second section of the questionnaire dealt with information technology development and administrative activities. It consisted of six questions. The respondent was presented with a five-point scale for each question and was asked to circle the appropriate score on the scale. Table 5.3 presents a descriptive summary of this section.

The third and last section dealt with the strategic alignment of information technology, control, and organizational structure. It consisted of seven questions. Table 5.4 provides a descriptive summary of this section.

Even though the questions contained in sections II and III of the questionnaire are not directly related to the research at hand, they shed some light on a number of vital concerns of IT managers such as the structure of the IT organization as well as organizational and top management commitment.

Table 5.3
Descriptive Summary of Section II of the Questionnaire

Scale	1	2	3	4	5
Question # 1^1	0^2	1	7	27	22
Question # 2	0	2	7	25	23
Question # 3	0	2	9	20	26
Question # 4	0	4	3	27	23
Question # 5	0	5	8	26	18
Question # 6	0	6	11	23	17

[1] These represent the number of respondents.

Table 5.4
Descriptive Summary of Section III of the Questionnaire

	Yes	No	Don't Know
Question # 1[1]	48[2]	5	4
Question # 2	47	10	n/a[3]
Question # 3	33	24	n/a
Question # 4	40	17	n/a
Question # 5	48	9	n/a
Question # 6	28	29	n/a
Question # 7	57	0	n/a

[1] The figures represent the respondents in each category.
[2] Not applicable.

RELATIVE COMPARATIVE INDEXES OF IT

From our discussion in the previous sections, it can be concluded that the decision of how much to invest in information technology has been a nagging question worrying IT managers and practitioners, not only in the United States, but globally in most developed countries. As was discussed earlier, empirical research has not reached conclusive results because of methodological, sampling, and data problems. Further, it was concluded that no strong relationship has been established between the level of investment in IT and the company's performance. In this section, an index is developed to measure IT performance that will be employed later to test empirically the hypotheses pertaining to the interaction between IT investment and performance. As discussed above, how heavily a company has invested in IT was evaluated in several ways. All appropriate measures, however, are necessarily dynamic, since they must be related to indicators of change in the firm's investment profile in a given area and over a period of time. Since the level of IT investments is industry-specific, its impact on performance can be evaluated through examining their "relative comparative advantage." Examining the observed pattern of investment according to this criterion allows the influences determining a company's IT comparative advantage to be taken into consideration without testing them directly.[2]

Relative advantage, in general, has been defined by Rogers (1983) as "the degree to which an innovation is perceived as being better than the idea it supersedes" (p. 213). The revealed comparative advantage criterion for a specific company boils down to developing an index that is obtained by dividing the company's "IT index" by the industry "IT index." The company's IT index is the ratio of the revenue generated in a specific year (this is the total revenue figure for the particular year) and the current book value of IT assets for the same year. This would yield the number of dollar income generated for each dollar invested in IT at one point in time. The industry's IT index is the average IT index for the whole industry. In other words, it is the ratio of the sum of total revenues of all companies in a particular industry and the sum of IT assets for the same companies. If the revealed IT index for a specific company is higher than one, then this company has an IT-related advantage over its competitors. In other words, it has a high IT performance vis-a-vis its competitors. On the another hand, if the revealed IT index is less than one, then the company is not benefiting from its IT investment, or it is not utilizing its IT appropriately to compete in the industry. Applying this concept on the 57 respondent companies resulted in 37 companies with an IT index of less than one and 20 companies with an IT index greater than one. This supports the argument that many companies have been overinvesting in information technology, or they may simply have not yet realized the benefits from their IT investments.

Based on the results of the Diebold study (1984), which found that the level of investment in information technology is industry-specific, industry specificity will be considered a determinant factor in IT investment and IT performance. In other words, a firm in the service sector is not expected to invest in IT at the same level as another firm in the manufacturing sector. Another factor that is believed to affect the level of investment in IT is the extent of control, both strategic and operational, top management would like to exercise on the company's activities.

To test the proposition that IT investment is industry-specific, a simple statistical test is conducted using the current value of IT investment as a dependent variable and industry type as an independent variable.

From Table 5.1 above, we can see that the number of industries in our sample is 11. Because the number of companies in each industry is not statistically large, these companies were classified in two categories (CATG). The first category (CATG = 1) contains companies in technology-intensive industries (such as aerospace, electronics, and computers), and the second category (CATG = 0) contains those companies that did not fit the criterion to be placed in the first category (examples in this category include food and metals). A t-test is conducted to test for any statistical difference between the two categories. The results of the t-test are presented in Table 5.5.

From Table 5.5, the value of the t-statistic is 0.0844, which is statistically significant at the 90 percent confidence level. Hence, it is concluded that investment in IT is industry-specific. The variable industry will be used as an independent variable in the multivariate analysis that follows.

The set of hypotheses to be tested in this chapter are:

H01b: Companies with relative IT advantage tend to have high equity ownership by managers.

H02b: Companies with relative IT advantage tend to have a higher ratio of inside to outside directors.

H03b: There exists a positive relationship between the size of the firm as measured by gross fixed assets and the company's relative IT index.

The dependent variable utilized in the statistical analysis is the information technology index (ITI) developed above:

ITI = 1 for firms with a relative information advantage index > 1
ITI = 0 for firms with a relative information advantage index < 1.

Table 5.5
Results of the T-Test for Industry Specificity

CATG	N	Mean	Std Err	Min	Max
0	28	0.182	0.39477	0	1
1	36	0.407	0.50071	0	0

T	DF	Prob > T
-1.7632	62	0.0844

IT INVESTMENT AND EQUITY OWNERSHIP

Using the "Relative IT Index" or the information technology index (ITI) concept and the indexes developed for the respondent companies, descriptive univariate statistics were developed for each category to determine if there were differences between companies that have relative IT advantage (with an IT index of one) and those which do not (with an IT index of zero). T-tests were conducted to determine if the differences were statistically significant.

Tables 5.6 and 5.7 demonstrate that both the total number of directors on the board (BOD) and the ratio of outside to inside directors (OBD) are statistically significant in differentiating between those companies that have a relative IT advantage and those that do not. Both variables are significant at the 95 percent confidence level.

Table 5.8 confirms our earlier indication that assets, used as a proxy for size, are a determining variable of the level of IT investment. As illustrated in Chapter 4, the variable asset was not found to be statistically significant because of the nonrandom sampling procedure employed there where companies in the experimental and control groups were matched based on size, thereby neutralizing any effect the variable gross assets might have had.

From Table 5.9, it is concluded that those companies where managers own a large percentage of stocks have relative IT advantage over other companies where management ownership is relatively lower. The value of the t-statistic is 0.0266, which falls well within the boundaries of the 95 percent confidence level.

Table 5.6
Variable = Nnmber of Directors (BOD)

ITI	N	Mean	Std Err	Min	Max
0	37	11.6222	0.4372652	5	18
1	20	13.3000	0.6286996	9	22
T		DF	Prob > T		
-2.1549		55	0.0350		

The results of the univariate tests indicate that the hypothesized relationships do exist. These tests are an important first step in data analysis, but multivariate tests assist in promoting understanding of the interactive effect of the combined independent variables.

Table 5.7
Variable = Ratio of Outside Directors (OBD)

ITI	N	Mean	Std Err	Min	Max
0	37	8.9111	0.37581	2	14
1	20	10.400	0.60437	6	19
T		DF	Prob > T		
-2.1497		55	0.0354		

Table 5.8
Variable = Gross Assets (GA)

ITI	N	Mean	Std Err	Min	Max
0	37	7.559	0.210644	5.407	10.306
1	20	8.256	0.268213	6.275	10.443
T		DF	Prob > T		
-1.9172		55	0.0597		

Table 5.9
Variable = Management Ownership (MO)

ITI	N	Mean	Std Err	Min	Max
0	37	5.865	1.113589	0.050	28.00
1	20	14.968	5.062699	0.400	87.70
T		DF	Prob. > T		
-2.2789		55	0.0266		

Logit analysis will be used to isolate those independent variables that have significant leverage on IT investment. As discussed extensively in Chapter 4, logit is appropriate when the dependent variable is discrete rather than continuous. Logit is a transformation in which the log of the odds of group membership is linearly related to the matrix of unknown parameter estimates.

The results of the stepwise logit analysis are presented in Table 5.10. As can be seen, the only two variables significant at the 90 percent confidence level are management ownership (MO) and the ratio of outside to inside board members (OBD). The other variables were excluded from the model. The p-value for the entire model is 0.0106 and the model Chi-square is 8.17 with 2 degrees of freedom.

The results of the logit analysis do not necessarily indicate that the variables that were excluded form the model do not have an impact on a company's relative IT advantage. As explained in Chapter 4, the problem of multicollinearity among the independent variables is the main reason why variables are shown to be statistically insignificant from the multivariate analysis. As can be seen from the matrix of correlation in Table 5.11, variables BOD, OBD, and GA are highly correlated. This is expected since firms with larger sizes are expected to have a larger number of directors on the board. Another problem presents itself in our case, that is, the size of the sample. Results from multivariate statistical analysis based on a small sample are always questionable. This is why we tend to place more reliance on the results from the univariate analysis.

Table 5.12 demonstrates that classification ability of the model. As

Table 5.10
Stepwise Logit Results

Variable	Beta	Std Err	Chi-Square	P
Intercept	-3.404585	1.334494	6.51	0.0107
MO	0.058772	0.029984	3.85	0.0500
OBD	0.235261	0.126011	3.49	0.0619

Notes:

N = 57.

Goodness of fit for the test: $G^2 = 64.78$. $G^2 = -2 \log (L_0 / L_1)$, where L_1 is the value of the likelihood function for the full model as fitted and L_0 is the maximum value of the likelihood function if all coefficients except the intercept are 0.

Table 5.11
Matrix Correlation of Independent Variables

	BOD	OBD	MO	GA
BOD	1.0000 0.0000	0.8835 0.0001	0.0132 0.9222	0.2464 0.0647
OBD		1.0000 0.0000	0.0144 0.9155	0.2600 0.0508
MO			1.0000 0.0000	-0.2475 0.0634
GA				1.0000 0.0000

can be seen, the model correctly classifies 77.2 percent of the observations.

SUMMARY

This chapter dealt with the question of IT investment and IT performance. The first section reviewed the thin literature on information technology and organizational performance. In particular, a number of empirical studies on the relationship between IT investment and performance were examined. It was concluded that the different studies reached conflicting or inconclusive results because of (1) the different proxies utilized to measure the level of IT investments, (2) the different indicators employed to measure performance, (3) the different data samples employed in the analysis, and (4) the different methodologies and methods utilized by the authors to collect their data and analyze it. These variations would result in different levels of validity and reliability, which in turn would lead to a diversity of research conclusions.

In order to improve research on IT performance analysis, Kathy Curley and John Henderson (1989) suggest that IT investment payoff be examined at four different levels: (1) the macroeconomic level, (2) the level of the firm or strategic business units (SBU), (3) the functional unit or the level of subgroups within an organization, departments, or project teams, and (4) the individual level, the most extensively studied to date.

Table 5.12
Classification Ability of the Logit Model

		Predicted		
		Negative	Positive	Total
True	Negative	37	0	37 (65%)
	Positive	13	7	20 (35%)
		50 (88%)	7 (12%)	57 (100%)

Sensitivity: 35.0%;   Specificity: 100%;   Correct: 77.2%;
False positive rate: 0.0%;   False negative rate: 26.6%.

An examination of the actual behavior of a number of organizations regarding the issue of IT investments and questions such as when to invest, where to invest, and how much to invest, leads one to conclude that in the absence of a set of standard guidelines and well-defined IT policies, an organization can overinvest in information technology. Information technology investments can be enhanced by the existence of a corporate policy that includes guidelines for major business activities that will require detailed procedures and standards to cover all IT issues.

The development and discussion of the questionnaire employed to collect the appropriate data for our analysis were presented in section three of this chapter. The questionnaire was created so that both quantitative and qualitative data would be relatively easy to collect and analyze. The questionnaire consisted of factual questions about pertinent factors, so that meaningful relationships between independent variables and dependent variable could be examined. Only structured questions were included in the survey instrument, in order to increase the response rate. Ninety percent of the respondents provided their names and their titles. The questionnaire was sent to 305 top information technology executives identified through *The Directory of Top Computer Executives* (1988).

Section four of this chapter developed a new indicator to measure

Section four of this chapter developed a new indicator to measure information technology performance. Based on the concept of comparative advantage, an index called "the information technology index" (ITI) was developed to measure the relative IT advantage of a company over its competitors. This ITI index is computed by dividing the company's "IT index" by the industry "IT index." The company's IT index is the ratio of the revenue generated in a specific year (this is the total revenue figure for the particular year) and the current book value of IT assets for the same year. This would yield the number of dollar income generated for each dollar invested in IT at one point in time. The industry's IT index is the average IT index for the whole industry. If the revealed IT index for a specific company is higher than one, then this company has an IT-related advantage over its competitors, and information technology is said to have high performance. In other words, it has a high IT performance vis-a-vis its competitors. On the another hand, if the revealed IT index is less than one, then the company is not benefiting from its IT investment, or it is not utilizing its IT appropriately to compete in the industry.

Empirical analysis utilizing primary data collected over a period of two years was conducted. It was demonstrated that there exists a positive relationship between the level of management ownership and the company's relative IT advantage. In the narrow framework, this is an interesting finding since it solidifies the argument of agency theory theorists that managers who own a large percentage of a company's stock pay more attention to the company's activities, in general, and IT investment, in particular, than those who don't. In the wider context, it outlines the relationship among firm control, management ownership, and information technology. As stated in Chapter 3, control is the purpose of agency and the basis for agency theory, and organizational control is one of the most fundamental and most important areas of management activities. Control means assuring that the principal's actions and work are performed by some people, and information technology strengthens managers' ability to control by communicating information rapidly across distances and by utilizing computational routines.

Managers, basically, have to protect their own interests as well as the interests of stockholders, and those who fail to anticipate, read, and respond to changes in their organization's vital signs will not be able to carry out their responsibilities well, if at all. Information technologies have been developed to ensure that managers obtain the appropriate information at the right time and to raise the process of managing from the level of piecemeal, spotty information, intuitive guesswork, and isolated problem solving to the level of systems insights, systems information, sophisticated data processing, and systems problem solving. This is why managers with large stock ownership tend to invest appropriately in information technology and tend to obtain the most benefit from their investments as was demonstrated in the empirical analysis.

The second finding of the chapter was that companies with a large number of outside directors on the board tend to have high relative IT advantage over their competitors. This is an expected finding, since the role of outside directors is to improve the board mechanism in monitoring managers, and agency theorists view the board of directors as a mechanism for reducing agency cost arising from the problem of separation of ownership (risk bearing) and control (management) in a corporation.

The third finding of the chapter (that companies in high-technology industries are more likely to invest more in information technology and to reap better benefits than those companies in other industries) is consistent with two previous studies: PIMS of 1984 and Strassmann of 1985.

NOTES

1. For an excellent study of IT investment and its relation to the firm's performance, see Weill and Olson (1989).

2. For a discussion of the concept of "relative comparative advantage," refer to Bella Belassa (1965, 1981).

6

Where Do We Go from Here?

This book explored the significant relationships between a company's management of and investment in information technology (IT) and the company's ownership structure, the board of directors, size, and financial characteristics.

Rapid progress is being made in the areas of information and information technology as a result of accelerated development of systems, products, and services. As these developments proceed, they are bringing with them productivity gains and improvements in industrial and business efficiencies. As a matter of fact, information and information technologies are "a major new force in the development of our economies and societies. The implications of this new force are so pervasive, so diverse, so radical, and so profound that almost no human action will remain untouched by them" (Bitterman 1989: 307).

This concluding chapter outlines the flow of the research that was undertaken during the study that formed the basis for this book. The purpose of this chapter is, first, to review and restate the research objectives of the study; second, to discuss briefly the methods employed in the research; and third, to summarize the empirical findings and sum up the answers to the primary and secondary research questions. These are to be followed by the major conclusions and implications drawn from the analysis. Finally, a number of recommendations are set forth along with suggestions for future research.

SUMMARY OF THE RESEARCH

Information technology is one of the major powers affecting the direction organizations are taking in our day, and numerous terms have been used to symbolize the change that has occurred in today's society. The recent explosion of information and information technology has induced corporate management to utilize its ingenuity in creating the best available means to manage the flow of information, control flow channels, and integrate the different assets (both hardware and software) of information technology utilized by the different divisions of the corporation.

To help organizations solve critical business problems and provide new services by the means of collecting data, turning data into information, and turning information into knowledge quickly enough to reflect its value, organizations are investing more and more in information technology (IT).

Although the role of information is perceived differently by different scholars, the fact that it constitutes an integral component of global business is no longer disputable. Practically, many American companies have adopted various approaches to information and information technology. These approaches are based on using information strategically, creating competitive opportunities, increasing the use of technology more effectively, and enhancing a more enduring connection between IT investments and strategic goals. Many businesses have accepted the notion that IT can play (and in fact is playing) a strategic role by creating competitive advantage rather than simply displacing cost.

To gain that competitive edge, these corporations have been using information technology in a variety of ways, such as the creation of interorganizational systems, which connect customers, suppliers, and competitors to the organization's computers, and origination of systems supporting strategic decisions, such as marketing analyses, cost management, control, and so on. To be able to address the need to build a competitive advantage, a company requires a strategy that addresses the what, why, how, and when of acquiring and using technical resources. To be effective, the IT strategy must be an integral component of the company's overall strategy, and must support the company's objectives and goals.

Economic globalization has affected information management in unexpected ways. The rapid growth of multinational corporations in both number and degree of influence has been accompanied by an unprecedented flow of information across international borders.

Managers in our day are utilizing information technology as a core element in aggressive new approaches to gain access to national and international marketplaces that were closed to them or to enhance control of internal operations. Those managers have, explicitly or implicitly, realized that, in the past few years, information technology has gone through a radical change. In reality, both the applications and the effective management of information technology look very different from what they did just a few years ago. Volatility in the business environment, coupled with technology's ability to provide management with efficient communication and information, is radically moving corporate management to realize that the "proactive" management of information and information technology is as critical as the management of other resources, if not more so. As a result, managers can no longer easily avoid the process of making decisions about information technology. IT affects the entire organization from its design and structure to product market strategies and to the way services are provided. Consequently, an increasing number of corporate leaders are buying into the idea that information and information technology are critical to the survival and success of their companies in the 1990s and into the next century. Corporate leaders have realized that information and information technology are value-adding ideas and not cost-containment ones, and that information technology is playing a major role in achieving productivity and quality.

A variety of benefits are provided by information technologies: better benefits, improved communications, an evolving understanding of information requirements, and cost reductions. The information provided by new advanced technology has characteristics that are important to management. It supports decision making by identifying areas that require attention, providing answers to questions, and giving knowledge about related areas. It provides relevant, timely information. In addition, information technology has improved communications in several ways. It is used to facilitate the sharing of information with customers and suppliers.

In 1958, Robert Slater wrote an article speculating about the impact of information technology on organizations. He foresaw a shift of operations to the electronic data processing department and more authority and influence of the data processing manager. Following in Slater's footsteps, many other researchers undertook the exercise of predicting the impact of information technology on various aspects of the work life, including economic, social, and political impacts.

One of the main advantages of information technology is its use to exploit internal and external competitive opportunities by the firm. The use of IT as a competitive weapon has been extensively covered in the literature. What has not received enough attention, however, is the equally dramatic but much less visible impact of the new technology on management control systems, both external and internal. The controlling function consists of actions and decisions managers undertake to ensure that actual results are consistent with desired results.

The logic is evident that information technology facilitates effective control. In any organization, managers are concerned that resources are productively deployed, job responsibilities properly stated, and various assignments adequately coordinated. To ensure that resources are used appropriately, managers develop structures and use such processes as planning, monitoring, and reporting to maintain control. With the advances in information technology, comprehensive control systems based on a global or corporate view are possible today.

By examining and analyzing the literature and the research performed on the subject of information technology, a missing ingredient was identified: No study has been carried out on the impact of company's ownership structure on top management commitment to management investing in information technology and its capitalizing on the new technology. Companies with widely held stocks and diverse stock ownership are believed to have a different levels of commitment to, investment in, and performance of information technology than companies with concentrated stock ownership. Further, it is also believed that companies where top managers are large stockholders would exercise a different level of control than companies where managers do not control a large percentage of the stock. Control is an intervening variable in the linkage between organizational ownership structure and information technology.

The primary objective of the study was to test, from an agency perspective, how different ownership structures impact on the way information technology is managed, on the one hand, and the level of investment in and performance of information technology, on the other. The research question the study sought to answer was: How does a company's ownership structure affect the level of IT investment and performance and the way IT is managed?

To support this primary research question, in addition to the variable ownership and the existence of a CIO, other variables were included in the analysis. Hypotheses were formulated based on the results of the literature search or for their relevance to the research.

Variables, such as size, financial characteristics, number of outside directors on the board, and so forth, were deemed appropriate in explaining some statistical variability.

HYPOTHESES AND METHODOLOGY

Two sets of testable hypotheses were developed, the first pertaining to the question of information technology management and the determinants leading to the appointment of a chief information officer (CIO) to head the IT department. The other set of hypotheses concerns the relationship between IT performance as measured by the "information technology index" (ITI) and a number of company-specific characteristics.

A cross-sectional matched-pair design was used to compare corporations that had a CIO on the top-level management executive team in 1988 to *similar* corporations that did not have one for the same year. The function of a matched-pair design is to control for factors in the samples that are being matched and to limit the effect of such controlled factors. Based on the variables that were matched, one sample from each different population was selected and matched together as one pair. In order to control the substantive differences in economic environments in different industries, the matched-pair factor was industry-specific. In other words, in order to minimize groupings in which firms have unrelated activities in an economic sense, the important point in the identification of similar firms was the Standard Industrial Classification (SIC).

A cross-sectional experimental design was utilized to test the hypotheses formulated. This is a type of correlational design, and is the simplest and most effective of the correlational designs in which all measurements are taken at one point in time. This cross-sectional approach is very useful in determining if two or more variables have any relationships and establishing those relationships.

The 108 corporations in the experimental group were selected from the list of the Fortune 500 industrial corporations that had a CIO on the top-level executive management team and made the Fortune 500 list in the past three years. The control group was composed of a set of 108 corporations from the population of 1988 Fortune 500 corporations that did not have a CIO on the top-level executive management team. The matching process of the experimental corporations was based upon the SIC and revenues. These criteria were designed to identify the most compatible control subjects.

In the current research, eight independent variables were identified as determinants of hiring a CIO on the top-level executive management team. These were management ownership structure (MO), book value of gross assets (GA), revenues (RE), number of employees (EM), capital intensity (CI), ratio of outside to inside directors on the board (OBD), CEO duality (DU), and industry structure (IS).

Both univariate and multivariate analyses were conducted. The purpose of univariate analysis was to identify any differences in characteristics between firms with a CIO and those without a CIO. For example, if the independent variable is company's GA, using univariate analysis will help us understand whether there is any difference between the two groups of firms with respect to this variable. On the other hand, multivariate analysis was employed to test the hypotheses formulated.

SUMMARY OF THE FINDINGS

As mentioned above, the analytic procedures used in investigating the research questions included the univariate t-test as well as the multivariate logit regression analysis. The eight independent variables included in the analysis of the management structure of IT were: management stock ownership, gross assets, revenues, number of employees, ratio of outside to inside directors on the board, duality, industry structure, and capital intensity of the company. The results of the univariate tests indicate that firms choosing to have a CIO on the top-level executive management team have different characteristics than those firms not electing to have a CIO in a top management position.

The objective of Chapter 4 was to identify those company-specific factors that affect the creation of a CIO executive position on the top-level management team to manage information and information technology in an organization. As discussed, information technology penetrates all formal and informal control systems in addition to acting as a control system by itself. It is argued that as managerial supervision increases (more effective control), the need for a well-managed informational system increases, hence the necessity for a top-level executive position to manage this informational system and act as a liaison between the various informational systems in the organization and the CEO and other executives.

A number of company-specific attributes were identified by the statistical analysis as significant determinants of the creation of a CIO top executive position where the CIO acts as an *informational control agent*; these characteristics were empirically identified as management equity ownership, industry structure, and the composition of the board of directors. The findings support the first hypothesis that if management equity ownership is high, managers will be more involved in the close monitoring of company's activities and the collection of information, and will be willing to appoint a CIO reporting directly to the CEO or the CFO. As was stated repeatedly throughout the book, the role of the CIO in a top executive position is to provide a relatively low-cost mechanism for assuring the survival of other members of the top management team, and decreasing the likelihood of their replacement or reordering. As a result, when the equity held by top management increases, their managerial supervision increases because of increased economic interest. The absence of a CIO might cause the sacrificing of managers' interests as stockholders. Empirically, and using both univariate and multivariate analyses, a statistically significant relationship was found between the existence of a top-level executive CIO and the level of management stock ownership.

The finding that companies with a relatively large number of outside directors tend to have a CIO in an executive position supports the premise of agency theory that more outside board members means better attention to stockholders' interests. Also, in order for outside board members to better serve their constituents, they need to have access to more timely information. As a result, they will push for better management of information technology resources and, consequently, the creation of a CIO position on the top-level executive management team.

Univariate and multivariate statistical analyses also revealed industry structure to be a differentiating variable between companies with a CIO on the top-level executive management team and those without. This result is not surprising since it is expected that companies operating in industries with different levels of technological developments, structures, and competitiveness would have varying information technology needs and would adopt different policies in managing their IT resources.

On the other hand, the study failed to support the hypothesis of agency cost as exemplified by the size of the corporation. This unexpected result is probably caused by the choice of the experimental and control groups. Since the choice of the corporations was based on a matched-pair design and the matching variable was size, the impact of this variable was neutralized by the selection process. In addition, since CI was measured as the ratio of GA and the number of employees (EM), its impact, if there is any, was also neutralized by the sample selection process. Capital- intensive production techniques involve a more advanced technological level and, consequently, the use of information technology in the production, running, and operating of the technology used. The more capital intensive the corporation, the more its reliance on information technology would be, and the higher the likelihood of appointing a CIO on the top-level executive management team. The CIO's role here is one of an "integrator" where he or she links the functions of the various departments. This research did not support the capital intensity hypothesis by finding a statistically insignificant association between the capital intensity of a corporation as measured by the ratio of fixed asset to total number of employees and the presence of a CIO on the top-level executive management team.

Another hypothesis that was not supported by the statistical analysis was that of the CEO duality. From a control perspective, management would have more command of the corporation and the way it was governed if the CEO served in a dual capacity. Hence, to assure board members that a CEO/chairperson dual role will not erode their control, management introduces an "assurance factor" by creating a CIO position on the top-level executive management team. The CIO in this capacity ensures the objectivity and reliability of information provided by the CEO.

Chapter 4, then, isolated three variables that aid in the explanation of the phenomenon of the creation of a CIO on the top-level executive management team. Two variables are related to the management of the company, management equity ownership and the composition of the board of directors; the third variable has to do with a structural component, the technological level of a corporation. The model correctly classified an approximate 65 percent of the companies in a sample of 108 matched-pair firms. Other variables were postulated to be strong candidates as potential determinants of a CIO top executive position, such as company size, which was used as a proxy for agency cost, and duality. These two variables, however, were not selected by the logit analysis model.

In Chapter 5 the question of IT investment and IT performance was examined. The review of the literature on information technology and performance revealed that this field of research is still in its infancy. A number of empirical studies on the relationship between IT investment and performance were examined. It was concluded that these different studies reached conflicting or inconclusive results because of (1) the different proxies utilized to measure the level of IT investments, (2) the different indicators employed to measure performance, (3) the different samples employed in the analysis, and (4) the different methodologies and methods utilized by the authors to collect their data and analyze it. These variations would result in different levels of validity and reliability, which in turn would lead to a diversity of research conclusions.

In order to improve research on IT performance analysis, Kathy Curley and John Henderson (1989) suggest that IT investment payoff be examined at four different levels: (1) the macroeconomic level, wherein gross economic aggregations may be employed to examine the impact of IT investment on the overall national economy; (2) the level of the firm or strategic business units (SBU), where concerns center on competitiveness and business strategy; (3) the functional unit or the level of subgroups within an organization, departments, or project teams. On this front, there have been two major findings. The first is that the most significant impacts of IT introduced into work groups have not been those originally anticipated. The second key finding has been that intangible benefits have not been translated into benefits to the organization as a whole; and (4) the individual level which has been the most extensively studied to date. Much of the research on this level has been concerned with IT impact on task-specific issues, such as the improvements of efficiency in data entry clerks or word processing staff as a result of new IT investments.

To enhance the acceptability and productivity of information technology, then, there is a need to develop an IT policy, at the corporate level, that is compatible with the overall objectives and goals of the corporation. Such a policy should (1) promote structural adjustments as a result of the introduction of new information technologies, (2) provide guidelines for education and training, and (3) ensure that the new IT resources are utilized in the most efficient manner.

An examination of the actual behavior of a number of organizations regarding the issue of IT investments and questions such as when to invest, where to invest, and how much to invest, leads one to conclude that in the absence of a set of standard guidelines and well-defined IT policies, an organization can be driven back on its own resources. Information technology investments can be enhanced by the existence of a corporate policy that includes guidelines for major business activities that will require detailed procedures and standards to cover all IT issues. Approaches to planning a strategy for issuing such a policy must take into consideration: (1) organizational goals and objectives, (2) organizational attributes, and (3) agreement with established organizational policies. Support for developing the policy should be given by the board of directors. In addition, organizational policies should include specific statements concerning such areas as organizational structure, performance, and funding.

The development and discussion of the questionnaire employed to collect the appropriate data for our analysis were also presented in Chapter 5. The questionnaire was created so that both quantitative and qualitative data would be relatively easy to collect and analyze. The questionnaire consisted of factual questions about pertinent factors so that meaningful relationships between independent variables and dependent variable could be examined. Only structured questions were included in the survey instrument, in order to increase the response rate. Ninety percent of the respondents provided their names and their titles.

In Chapter 5, also, a new indicator to measure information technology performance was developed. Based on the concept of comparative advantage, an index called "the information technology index" (ITI) was developed to measure the relative IT advantage of a company over its competitors. This ITI index is computed by dividing the company's "IT index" by the industry "IT index." The company's IT index is the ratio of the revenue generated in a specific year (this is the total revenue figure for the particular year) and the current book value of IT assets for the same year. This would yield the number of dollar income generated for each dollar invested in IT at one point in time. The industry's IT index is the average IT index for the whole industry. In other words, it is the ratio of the sum of total revenues of all companies in a particular industry and the sum of IT assets for the same companies. If the revealed IT index for a specific company is higher than one, then this company has an IT-related advantage over its competitors, and information technology is said to have high performance. In other words, it has a high IT performance vis-a-vis its competitors. On the another hand, if the revealed IT index is less than one, then the company is not benefiting from its IT investment, or it is not utilizing its IT appropriately to compete in the industry.

Empirical analysis utilizing primary data collected over a period of two years was conducted. It was demonstrated that there exists a positive relationship between the level of management ownership and the company's relative IT advantage. In the narrow framework, this is an interesting finding, since it solidifies the argument of agency theory theorists that companies where managers own a large percentage of stocks pay more attention to the company's activities, in general, and IT investment, in particular. In the wider context, it outlines the relationship among firm control, management ownership, and information technology.

As the size and complexity of corporations increased, it became necessary to incorporate multilevel, multidimensional organizational control systems. Modern information technology is dramatically improving the quality of organizational control by integrating the different control systems. Control of the firm is vital when decision makers (managers) are the main shareholders. Under such circumstances, managers shoulder a heavy portion of the wealth effects resulting from their decisions, and they may be more likely to make decisions that are in the best interest of the shareholders. In addition, if managers are to be accountable for their actions and the actions of their subordinates, and if they are to carry out their control responsibilities in an effective and efficient manner, they require ready access to current information concerning what, when, and how things have transpired in their spheres of influence. Information technology strengthens managers' ability to control by communicating information rapidly across distances and by utilizing computational routines.

Managers, basically, have to protect their own interests as well as the interests of stockholders, and those who fail to anticipate, read, and respond to changes in their organization's vital signs will not be able to carry out their responsibilities well, if at all. Information technologies have been developed to ensure that managers obtain the appropriate information at the right time and to raise the process of managing from the level of piecemeal, spotty information, intuitive guesswork, and isolated problem solving to the level of systems insights, systems information, sophisticated data processing, and systems problem solving. This is why managers with large stock ownership tend to invest appropriately in information technology and tend to obtain the most benefits from their investments as was demonstrated from the empirical analysis.

The second finding of the chapter was that companies with a large number of outside directors on the board tend to have a high relative IT advantage over their competitors. This is an expected finding, since the role of outside directors is to improve the board mechanism for monitoring managers. Agency theorists view the board of directors as a mechanism for reducing agency cost arising from the problem of separation of ownership (risk bearing) and control (management) in a corporation. Since most corporations in the United States are run by a team of executives who own a fraction of the firm's stock, management does not completely bear the negative consequences of any non-value-maximizing behavior in which it engages in. The board of directors is one mechanism employed to control this non-value-maximizing behavior of management. By acting as an information system to stockholders, the board is carrying out of its chief responsibility of managing the corporation and protecting the interests of the stockholders.

In recent years, increasing importance has been attached to the inclusion on the board of large corporations of individuals who were not officers of the company and who could thus have a view independent of that of corporate officers. It is important to recognize that agency theory places a heavy weight on outside members of the board of directors in implementing the board's role as an arm for strategic control, especially the setting of guidelines for implementation of effective control measures. It is with this duty that sophisticated information technology is utilized. Although existing literature does not fully define the content of the board's role in strategic control, advocates believe that it becomes obvious at those critical points when important decisions must be made. In addition, increased litigation from shareholders and consumer activists has focused attention on the role of the outside members of the board of directors and the fulfillment of their responsibilities. Various factors are shaping a contemporary stance, that holds that directors' primary responsibility is to the shareholders but recognizes that directors must give appropriate weight to the claims of other interested constituents of the firm. To fulfill those added responsibilities, directors must possess more timely and accurate information, and this strengthens the case for more investment in information technology.

The third finding of the chapter (that companies in high-technology industries are more likely to invest more in information technology and to reap better benefits than those companies in other industries) is consistent with two previous studies: PIMS of 1984 and Strassman of 1985.

FUTURE RESEARCH

One limitation of the study is that in the current research the analysis was cross-sectional. Static data was used to test for what are undoubtably dynamic relationships. Longitudinal analysis would have been more beneficial, but unfortunately, the lack of comprehensive longitudinal data on IT investment and stock ownership structure precluded such analysis. Studying firms at different points in time may help identify how changes in the independent variables affect the decisions on both management of and investment in information technology.

Another limitation is that the use of the Fortune 500 list of industrial companies is not a randomly chosen set of firms; as a matter of fact, this list consists of giant U.S. corporations. An extension of this study would be to examine the management of, investment in, and performance of information technology in smaller firms. Such an extension would make the results more generalizable.

A profound analysis might be made on an individual industry level, when and if data are available. In the case of the aerospace industry, for instance, where investment in information technology is massive, a perfect application would be to study the 17 largest Fortune 500 aerospace companies. Another example would be the pharmaceutical industry. Such industry-level studies help in the isolation of industry-specific characteristics and peculiarities of the different groups of companies.

Another recommendation for future research would be to study the relationship between company ownership structures and IT in other countries, for example the United Kingdom, Germany, France, and Japan. However, this recommendation is somehow more difficult to bring to life in the near future because of the less-than-acceptable coverage of existing data bases of foreign companies. For any study to be fruitful and professionally acceptable, information would have to be collected through questionnaires and over a long period of time. This is a lengthy and costly process, but it is professionally challenging.

A possible extension of this study is to examine the creation of a CIO position on the top-level management team in light of the structure and complexity of the organization. As the corporation becomes more complex, the need for a top-level information officer will increase. Although there are several aspects of organizational complexity, Hall (1973) identifies three basic components that he considers collectively: horizontal differentiation, vertical differentiation, and special dispersion.

Another proposition explored in this study concerned the impact of board composition on the creation of a top-level executive CIO position. It was suggested that as the ratio of outside board members increases, the likelihood for a CIO top executive position will increase. Strong support emerged for this proposition from the findings. If we accept the agency theory premise that low managerial equity interests diminish executives' commitment to stockholders' interests and heighten the importance of a board's governance role, this observation suggests that a board's tenure distribution is very critical for its ability to stand up against top management and requires more information and assurance of its objectivity. As suggested by Kosnik (1990: 147), outside directors' backgrounds and careers might be extremely relevant to the board's relationship with top management. This study could be expanded by including directors' backgrounds and careers as an additional explanatory variable.

Questions that might be raised and answered in future research involve such issues as the relationship between board composition and CEO duality. Other potential explanatory variables could be included in the analysis, such as the region of the country, age of the firm, maturity of the industry, nature of corporate strategy, and so on.

This study has isolated and analyzed one aspect of a very broad, rich, and complicated subject, that is, the management of information technology and its relation to the ownership structure of the corporation.

Many researchers are now investigating and questioning the benefits of large investment in, and performance of, information technology and the way it is managed. In the past 20 years, information technology literature has been filled with discussions of the types of impact from IT. Among the impacts investigated are changes in organizational structure, changes in labor force composition, shifts in the location of decision making and authority, impact on productivity, and so forth.

However, almost all researchers and practitioners agree that assessing the economic impacts of IT has been greatly hindered by the lack of reliable and accessible data. Two problems exits in this respect that prevent the possibility of multiple studies building on each other. The first problem is that most of the data are unavailable for analysis by other researchers. The second problem concerns inconsistency across data sources with respect to the data collected. As a matter of fact, deciding what data to collect is much more difficult than collecting data. In general, many American firms have not tracked investments and expenditures on IT separate from other areas. The information is usually combined with general operating and capital investment information. Recent action, however, by their Financial Accounting Standards Boards provides a beginning for the standardized tracking of IT investments.

Finally, the value of this research could be enhanced if it were replicated for other developed countries. Such a replication would make it possible to compare information management, control, and ownership structures in other developed economies, and would facilitate the task of formulating a global perspective on this important question.

Appendix I

Companies in the Experimental Group

McDonnell Douglas
Lockheed
General Dynamics
Textron
Northrop
Grumman
Rohr Industries
Claiborne (Liz)
Pepsico
Coca-Cola
Seagram (Jos. E.)
Owens-Corning Fiber
Manville
Corning Glass Works
Norton
National Gypsum
Dupont (E. I.) De Nemours
Monsanto
Grace (W. R.)
FMC
Ethyl
Air Products & Chemicals
Morton Thiokol
Nalco Chemical
IBM

James River
Scott Paper
Mead
Boise Cascade
Willamette Industries
Sonoco Products
Bemis
Leggett & Platt
Miller (Herman)
Deere
Harnischfeger Ind.
Triangle Industries
Combustion Engineering
Ball
Bethlehem Steel
Carpenter Technology
Inland Steel
Chrysler
Fruehauf
Exxon
Shell Oil
Ashland Oil
Amerada Hess
Pennzoil
Murphy Oil

Control Data
Pitney Bowes
Amdahl
Prime Computer
Data General
Tandem Computers
General Electric
TRW
Emerson Electric
Texas Instruments
North American Philips
National Semiconductor
Harris
Advanced Micro Dev.
Allegheny International
Scientific Atlanta
Sara Lee
Conagra
Archer Daniels
Pillsbury
Ralson Purina
General Mills
Quaker Oats
Campell Soup
Tyson Foods
International Multifoods
Mccormick
Champion International
Borden

Valero Energy
Merck
American Home Prod.
Pfizer
Abbott Laboratories
Warner-Lambert
Squibb
Robins (A. H.)
Donnelly (R. R.)
McGraw-Hill
Washington Post
Deluxe
Macmillan
Rubbermaid
Cooper Tire & Rubber
Bausch & Lomb
Bard (C. R.)
Colgate-Palmolive
Clorox
International Flavors
Armstrong World Ind.
Springs Industries
Fieldcrest Cannon
DWG
United Merchants
Philip Morris
Hasbro
Mattel
NCR

Appendix II

Companies in the Control Group

Boeing
Masco
Caterpillar
Sundstrand
Cummings Engine
Hartmax
Kellwood
Oxford Industries
Phillips Van Heusen
Ownes-Illinois
USG
Lafarge
Certainteed
Dow Chemical
Cameron Iron Work
American Cynamid
Hercules
Vulcan Materials
Engelhard
Nerco
General Motors
Pennwalt
Lubrizol
Gaf
Dexter

Fedcral Paper Board
Kerr-McGee
Potlatch
Dresser Industries
Consolidated Papers
Ingersoll-Rand
Black & Decker
Dover
Timken
Clark Equipment
Dennison Mfg.
Mapco
Briggs & Stratton
Coleman
Crown Central
Jostens
Aluminuim Co. of America
Quaker State
Louisiana Land & Exp.
Flowers Industries
Shaw Industries
Ford Motor
Dana
Paccar
Universal Food

Fuller (H. B.)
Echlin
Smith (A. O.)
Apple Computers
Lilly (Eli)
Compaq Computers
Schering-Plough
Westinghouse Electric
Motorola
Whirlpool
Cooper Industries
Intel
AMP
Loral
E-Systems
National Service Ind.
Varian Associates
Raychem
Champian Spark Plug
RJR Nabisco
Heinz (H. J.)
CPC Int'l
Kellog
Hormel (Geo. A.)
Dean Foods
Wilson Foods
Procter & Gamble
West Point-Pepperell
Emhart

Arvin Industries
American Brands
Kimberley-Clark
Johnson & Johnson
Stone Container
Great North Nebraska
Union Camp
Upjohn
Rorer Group
Gannett
Louisiana-Pacific
Tribune
Knight-Rider
American Greetings
Media General
Bowater
Esselte Business System
Jefferson Smurfit
Fleetwood Enterprises
Anheuser Busch
Xerox
Minnesota Mining
Polaroid
Time Inc.
Tektronix
EG&G
Brown-Forman
Gilette
Snap-On Tools

References

Aldrich, J., & Nelson, F. 1984. *Linear Probability, Logit, and Probit Models*. London: Sage Publications.

Alexander, J. A., & Fennell, M. L. 1986. "Patterns of Decision Making in Multihospital Systems," *Journal of Health and Social Behavior*, 27: 14-27.

Allen, B. 1990. "Information as an Economic Commodity," *American Economic Association*, 80(2): 268-273.

Alsup, R.G. 1987. "The Information Needs of the Savings and Loan Director," *Financial Managers' Statement* 9(2): 48-50.

Alter, Allan E. 1989. "An Interview with Tom Peters," *CIO Magazine*, August: 15-18.

Amihud, Y., & Lev, B. 1981. "Risk Reduction as a Managerial Motive for Conglomerate Mergers," *Bell Journal of Economics*, 12: 605-616.

Anderson, E. 1985. "The Salesperson as Outside Agent of Employee: A Transaction Cost Analysis," *Marketing Science*, 4: 234-254.

Argawal, A., & Mandelker, G. 1987. "Managerial Incentives and Corporate Investment and Financing Decisions," *Journal of Finance*, 42: 823-837.

Baginski, S. 1986. *Intra-Industry Information Transfer Associated with Management Earnings Forecasts*. Unpublished Ph.D. Dissertation, University of Illionois at Urbana-Champaign.

Barney, J. 1988. "Agency Theory, Employee Stock Ownership and a Firm's Cost of Equity Capital," Unpublished Working Paper, Texas A&M University, College Station.

Baysinger, B. D., Kosnik, R. D., & Turk, T. A. 1991. "Effects of Board and Ownership Struture on Corporate R&D Strategy," *Academy of Management Journal*, 34(1): 205-214.

Belassa, B. 1965. "Trade Liberalization and Revealed Comparative Advantage," *Manschaster Journal of Economics and Social Studies*, 33(2): 99-123.

————. 1981. "Trade in Manufacturing Goods: Patterns of Change," *World Development*, 9: 263-275.

Bender, D. 1986. "Fiancial Impact of Information Processing," *Journal of MIS*, 3(2): 232-238.

Berle, A., & Means, G. 1932. *The Modern Corporation and Private Property*. New York: Commerce Clearing House.

Bitterman, M. 1989. "Conclusions from TIDE II." In *Information Technology and Global Interdependence*, pp. 307-308.

Boddy, D. 1981. "Micro-Electronics and the Experience of Work," *HRD International*, 51-54.

Borbely, J. 1985. "Chief Information Officers: What's in a Title?" *Online*, 91-93.

Brown, B. 1988. "Texas Instrument Puts Final Touch on EDI Project," *Network World*, April 4: 2, 8.

Buchanan, D.A., & Boddy, D. 1983. *Organizations in the Computer Age*. Hampshire, U.K.: Gower Publishing.

Buchanan, J. R., & Linowes, R. G. 1980. "Understanding Distributed Data Processing," *Harvard Business Review*, July-Aug.: 108-15.

Buday, R. S. 1987. "In Search of an MIS Chief Who Truly Functions as a CIO," *Information Week*, May 25: 22-23, 26.

Burch, J. G., Strater, F. R., & Grudnitski, G. 1983. *Information Systems: Theory and Practice*. New York: John Wiley.

Burlingame, J. F. 1961. "Information Technology and Decentralization," *Harvard Business Review*, Nov.-Dec.: 89-97.

Busha, C.H., & Harter, S.P. 1980. *Research Methods in Librarianship: Techniques and Interpretation*. New York: Academic Press.

Business Week, 1984. "GM Moves into a New Era," July 16: 48-52, 54.

———— . 1984. "The Shape of Banking," June 18: 104-108, 110.

Campbell, T.S., & Kracaw, W.A. 1985. "The Market for Managerial Labor Services and Capital Market Equilibrium," *Journal of Financial and Quantitative Analysis*, 20: 277-97.

Carlyle, R.E. 1987. "Leading IS Shops Shifting to Centralized Structure," *Datamation*, 17-19.

Cash, J.I., McFarlan, F.W., & McKinney, J.L. 1983. *Corporate Information System Management: Text and Cases*. Homewood, IL: Irwin.

Child, J. 1984. "New Technology and Development in Management Organization," *Omega*, 12(3): 211-23.

Chow, C. 1983. "Empirical Studies of the Economic Impacts of Accounting Regulations: Findings, Problems and Prospects," *Journal of Accounting Literature*, 73-109.

CIO Magazine, 1990. "Top Corporate Executives,", January: 34-42.

Clifton, R. 1981. "A Strategic Overview of Business Information Systems," *Managerial Planning*, 29: 28-37.

Computerworld, 1989. "Speaks Softly, Carries a Big Stick," June 19, 57-61.

_____ . 1989. "Survey of CIOs," April 17, 1989: 75-78.

Cron, W., & Sobol, M. 1983. "The Relationship Between Computerization and Performance: A Strategy of Maximizing Economic Benefits of Computerization," *Information and Management*, 6: 171-181.

Cubbin, J., & Leech, D. 1983. "The Effect of Shareholder Dispersion on the Degree of Control in British Companies: Theory and Measurement," *Economic Journal*, 93: 351-369.

Curley, K., & Henderson, J. 1989. "Evaluating Investments in Information Technology," Working Paper, Sloan School of Management, MIT, Cambridge, MA.

Cusack, S. 1990. "Keeping Centralization on Track," *Computerworld*, 24 # 26: 67, 70.

Dalton, Dan. R., & Kesner, I. F. 1987. "Composition and CEO Duality in Boards of Directors: An International Perspective," *Journal of International Business Studies*, Fall: 33-42.

Datamation. 1986, 1987. "Data Processing Budget Study," *Datamation*.

Davis, G., & Olson, M. 1985. *Management Information Systems: Conceptual Foundations, Structure and Development*. New York: McGraw Hill.

Dawson, P., & McLaughlin, I. 1986. "Computer Technology and the Redefinition of Supervision," *Journal of Management Studies*, 23: 116-132.

Delone, W. H. 1988. "Determinants of Success for Computer Usage in Small Business, " *MIS Quarterly*, 12(1): 51-61.

Demsetz, H., & Lehn, K. 1985. "The Structure of Corporate Ownership: Theory and Consequences," *Journal of Political Economy*, 93: 1155-1177.

Demsetz, H. 1983. "The Structure of Ownership and the Theory of the Firm," *Journal of Law and Economics*, 26: 375-390.

Diebold Group, 1982, 1984. *MIS/Telecommunications Budgets and Key Indicators*. New York: The Diebold Group.

Directory of Top Computer Executives. East and West Editions. (Phoenix, AZ: Applied Computer Research, 1988).

Donovan, J. 1989. "From the Back Room to the Boardroom," *Computerworld*, April 17: 83-84.

Drucker, P. F. 1980. "Managing the Information Explosion," *The Wall Street Journal*, April 10: 24.

————. 1988. "The Coming of the New Organization," *Harvard Business Review*, Jan.-Feb.: 45-53.

DuPlessis, D.R. & Trenholm, B.A. 1991. "The Board of Directors: How Liable?" *CMA Magazine* 65(2): 27-30.

Easterbrook, F.H. 1984. "Two Agency-Cost Explanations of Dividends," *The American Economic Review*, 74:650-59.

Eccles, R. 1985. "Transfer Pricing as a Problem of Agency." In J. Pratt & R. Zeckhauser (eds.), *Principals, and Agents: The Structure of Business*, pp. 151-186. Boston: Harvard Business School Press.

Ein-Dor, P., & Segev, E. 1982. "Organizational Context and MIS Structure: Some Empirical Evidence," *MIS Quarterly*, September: 55-68.

Eizenhardt, K. M. 1989. "Agency Theory: An Assessment and Review," *Academy of Management Journal*, 14, 1: 57-74.

————. 1988. "Agency and Institutional Explanantions of Compensation is Retail Sales," *Academy of Management Journal*, 31: 488-511.

————. 1985. "Control: Organizational and Economic Approaches," *Management Science*, 31: 134-149.

Evans, Christopher, 1980. *The Micro Millenium*. New York: Viking Press.

Fama, Eugene F. 1980. "Agency Problems and the Theory of the Firm," *Journal of Political Economy*, 88: 288-307.

Fama, Eugene F. & Jensen, M. C. 1983. "Separation of Ownership and Control," *Journal of Law and Economics*, 23: 301-24.

Fayol, H. 1949. *General and Industrial Management*. London: Pitman Publishers.

Fiderio, J. 1987. "Managing Technology Portfolios," *Computerworld*, 21, 8: 77,79-80.

Fosberg, R. 1989. "Outside Directors and Managerial Monitoring," *Akron Business and Economic Review*, 20, 2: 24-32.

Galbraith, J.K. 1967. *The New Industrial State*. New York : New American Library.

Guimaraes, T., Farrell, C., & Song, J. 1988. "Computing Technology as a Strategic Business Tool," *SAM Advanced Management Journal*, Summer: 25-33.

Hall, Richard H. 1973. *Organizations: Structure and Process*. Englewood Cliffs, NJ: Prentice Hall.

Harris, S. E., & Katz, J. L. 1988. "Profitability and Information Technology Capital Intensity in the Insurance Industry." In *Proceedings of the Twenty-First Hawaii International Conference on System Sciences*, Vol. IV: 124-30.

Harvey, D. 1989. "Can IT Investments Be Made to Work?" *Director* 43, 1: 76-77.

Heckerman, D. 1975. "Motivating Managers to Make Investment Decisions," *Journal of Financial Economics*, 273-92.

Hector, G. 1988. "Yes, You Can Manage Long Term," *Fortune*, August: 64-76.

Hill, C.W.L. & Snell, S.A. 1989. "Effects of Ownership Structure and Control on Corporate Productivity," *Academy of Management Journal*, 32, 1: 25-46.

Holt, D. H. 1990. *Management: Principles and Practices*. Englewood Cliffs, NJ: Prentice Hall.

Hopper, Max D. 1990. "Rattling SABRE--New Ways to Compete on Information," *Harvard Business Review*, May-June: 118-25.

Houdeshel G., & Watson, H. J. 1987. "The Management Information and Decision Support System at Lockheed-Georgia," *MIS Quarterly*, 11, 1.

Huber, G. P. 1984. "The Nature and Design of Post-Industrial Organizations," *Management Sciences*, 30(8): 928-51.

Huber, G. P., & McDaniel, R. R. 1986. "The Decision Making Paradigm of Organizational Design," *Management Science*, 32(5): 572-89.

Huber, G. P. 1990. "A Theory of the Effects of Advanced Information Technologies on Organizational Design, Intelligence, and Decision Making," *Academy of Management Review*, 15, 1: 47-71.

Huff, S. 1990. "Evaluating Investments in Information Technology." *Business Quarterly*, 54 # 4: 42-45.

Jensen, Michael C., & Meckling, William H., 1976. "Theory of the Firm: Managerial Behavior, Agency Costs and Ownership Structure, *Journal of Financial Economics*, 3: 305-60.

Jussawalla, M.; Okuma, T.; & Araki, T. 1989. *Information Technology and Global Interdependence*. New York: Greenwood Press.

Karake, Zeinab A. 1990. "International Market Analysis Through Electronic Databases." In Grub, P., & Moran, R. (eds.) *Global Business Management in the 1990s*, pp. 462-66. Washington, D.C.: Beacham Publishing.

Kesner, Idalene F. & Dalton, Dan. R. 1986. "Boards of Directors and the Checks and (Im)balances of Corporate Governance," *Business Horizons*, October: 17-23.

Kosnik, Rita D., 1987. "Greenmail: A Study of Board Performance in Corporate Governance," *Administrative Science Quarterly*, 32: 163-85.

_____ . 1990. "Effects of Board Demography and Directors' Incentives on Corporate Greenmail Decisions," *Academy of Management Journal*, 33: 129-50.

Kreitner, R. 1990. *Management*. Boston: Houghton Mifflin.

Landau, Robert M. 1980. *Information Resources Management*. New York: AMACOM.

Laudon, K. C. & Laudon-Price, J. 1991. *Business Information Systems: A Problem-Solving Approach*. Hindale, IL: Dryden Press.

Leavitt, H.J., & Whisler, T.L. 1958. "Management in the 1980s," *Harvard Business Review*, 36 # 6: 41-48.

Linder, M. 1989. *Organizational Change and Information Technology*. Unpublished Doctoral Dissertation, the Harvard Business School.

Lucas, H.C., Jr. 1975. "The Use of an Accounting Information System, Action and Organizational Performance," *The Accounting Review*, 4: 735-746.

Maddala, G.S. 1983. *Econometrics*. New York: McGraw-Hill.

Manne, H.G. 1965. "Mergers and the Market for Corporate Control," *Journal of Political Economy*, 73: 110-20.

Masson, R. 1971. "Executive Motivations, Earnings and Consequent Equity Performance," *Journal of Political Economy* 79: 1278-292.

McFarlan, F. W., & McKenney, J. L. 1983. *Corporate Information Systems Management: The Issues Facing Senior Executives*. Homewood, IL: Dow Jones Irwin.

McFarlan, W. 1987. "How Information Technology is Changing Management Control Systems," *Harvard Business Review*, Note # 9-187-139.

McKinsey, J.D. 1922. *Organization*. New York: Ronald Press.

McIntyre, K.J. 1988. "Mather Learns From Early RMIS Setback," *Business Insurance*, 22(16): 155.

Meltzer, Morton F. 1981. *Information: The Ultimate Management Resource*. New York: AMACOM.

Miles, Ian, 1989. "Social Implications of Information Technology." In Jussawala, Okuma, & Araki (eds.) *Information Technology and Global Interdependence*. pp. 222-35. New York: Greenwood.

Miller, M., & Rock, K. 1985. "Dividend Policy under Asymmetric Information," *Journal of Finance*, December: 112-25.

Mintzberg, H. 1979. *The Structuring of Organizations*. Englewood Cliffs, NJ: Prentice Hall.

––––––––––. 1983. *Power in and Around Organizations*. Englewood Cliffs, NJ: Prentice Hall.

Mizruchi, Mark S. 1983. "Who Control Whom? An Examination of the Relation Between Management and Boards of Directors in Large American Corporations," *Academy of Management Review*, 8: 426-35.

Morck, R., Shleifer, A., & Vishny, R.W. 1986. "Management Ownership and Market Valuation: An Empirical Analysis," *Journal of Fianancial Economics* (Netherlands), 20(1,2): 293-315.

Morris, R. 1964. *The Economic Theory of Managerial Capitalism*. London: Macmillan.

––––––––––. 1987. "Signalling, Agency Theory, and Accounting Policy Choice," Accounting and Business Research, April: 47-56.

Murdick, R.G., & Ross, J.E. 1977. *Introduction to Management Information Systems*.

Myers, S., & Majluf, N. 1984. "Corporate Financing and Investment Decisions When Firms Have Information That Investors Do Not Have," *Journal of Financial Economics*, 13: 187-221.

Naisbitt, J. 1982. *Megatrends*. New York: Warner Books.

Netter, J., Wasserman, W., & Kutner, M. 1989. *Applied Linear Regression Models*. Homewood, IL: Irwin.

Neubarth, M. 1964. "MIS Needs Flexibility as Business Changes," *MIS Week*, 9, 20: 1.

Ogura, K. 1989. "Information Technologies and International Relations." In Jussawalla, Okuma, & Araki (eds.) *Information Technology and Global Interdependence*, pp. ix-xiii. New York: Greenwood.

Olson, M.H., & Chervany, N.L. 1980. "The Relationship Between Organizational Characteristics and the Structure of Information Services Function," *MIS Quarterly*, June: 57-68.

Orsey, Robert R. 1982. "Business Systems Planning: Management of Information," *Computer Horizons*, 14, 2: 154-56.

Ouchi, W.G. 1977. "The Relationship Between Organizational Structure and Organizational Control," *Administrative Science Quarterly*, 22(2): 95-113.

Ovalle, N.K. 1984. "Organizational/Managerial Control Processes: A Reconceptualization of the LInkage Between Technology and

Performance," *Human Relations*, 37, 12: 1047-62.

Parker, M. M., Trainor, H. E., & Benson, R. J. 1989. *Information Strategy and Economics*. Englewood Cliffs, NJ: Prentice Hall.

Passino, J. H., Jr., & Severance, D. G. 1988. "The Changing Role of the Chief Information Officer," *Planning Review*, Sept.-Oct.: 38-42.

Perrow, C. 1986. *Complex Organization*. New York: Random House.

Peters, T. 1988. "Restoring American Comptetiveness: Looking for New Models of Organizations," *Academy of Management Executive*, May: 99-108.

Pfeffer, J., & Leblebici, H. 1977. "Information Technology and Organizational Culture," *Pacific Sociological Review*, 20(2): 241-61.

Pfeffer, J., & Salanick, G.R. 1978. *The External Control of Organizations: A Resource Dependence Perspective*. New York: Harper and Row.

PIMS Program. 1984. *Management Productivity and Information Technology*. The Strategic Planning Institute, Cambridge, MA.

"Planning an IS Eurostrategy," *Information Week*, January 9, 1989.

Polilli, S. 1990. "Cost-Cutting Pressure on MIS Rising," *Software Magazine*. July: 23-25.

Porter, M. E., & Miller, V. E. 1985. "How Information Gives You Competitive Adavantage," *Harvard Business Review*, April: 149-60.

Pratt, J., & Zeckhauser, R. (eds.) 1985. *Principals and Agents: The Structure of Business*, Boston: Harvard Business School Press.

Press, S., & Wilson, S. 1978. "Choosing Between Logistic Regression and Discriminant Analysis," *Journal of The American Statistical Association*, December: 699-705.

Rechner, Paula L., & Dalton, D. R. 1989. "The Impact of CEO as Board Chairperson on Corporate Performance: Evidence vs. Rhetoric," *The Academy of Management Executives*, 3(2): 141-43.

Reeves, T. K., & Woodward, J. 1970. "The Study of Managerial Control." In J. Woodward (Ed.), *Industrial Organization: Behaviour and Control*. pp. 37-56. London: Oxford University Press.

Robey, D. 1977. "Computers and Management Structure: Some Empirical Findings Reexamined," *Human Relations*, 30(11): 963-76.

Rockart, J. F. 1979. "Chief Executives Define Their Own Data Needs," *Harvard Business Review*, March-April: 81-93.

————. 1988. "The Line Takes the Leadership--IS Management in a Wired Society," *Sloan Management Review*, Summer: 57-64.

Rogers, E. 1983. *Diffusion of Innovation*. New York: Free Press.

Securities and Exchange Commission, 1980. "Staff Report on Corporate Accountability," Washington, D.C., Government Printing Office, SEC.

Shoebridge, A. 1986. "The Use of Information Technology in the Boardroom," *Management Accounting*, 64(11): 20-22.

Siegman, T., & Karsh, B. 1962. "Some Organizational Correlates White Collar Automation," *Sociological Inquiry*, 32: 108-16.

Simon, H. A. 1977. *The New Science of Management Decisions*. Englewood Cliffs, NJ: Prentice Hall.

Singh, H., & Harrianto, F. 1989. "Management-Board Relationships, Takeover Risks, and the Adoption of Golden Parachutes," *Academy of management Journal*, 32: 7-24.

Singleton, J.P., McLean, E.R., & Altman, E.N. 1988. "Measuring Information Systems Performance: Experience with the Management by Results System at Security Pacific Bank," *MIS Quarterly*, 12(2): 325-37.

Slater, Robert E. 1958. "Thinking Ahead: How Near Is the Automatic Office?" *Harvard Business Review*, March-April:

Snow, M., & Jussawalla, M. 1989. "Deregulatory Trends in OECD Countries." In M. Jussawalla, Okuma, & Araki (eds.) *Information Technology and Global Interdependence*, pp. 21-39. New York: Greenwood Publishers.

Snyder, C. A., & Zienert L. A. 1990. "Telecommunications for Competitive Advantage: The Enterprise Network." In M. Khosrowpour & G. Yaverbaum (eds.). *Information Technology Resources Utilization and Management*, pp. 119-155. Harrisburg, PA: Idea Group Publishing.

Sprague, R.H. & McNurlin, B.C. 1986. *Information Management Systems in Practice*. Englewood Cliffs, NJ: Prentice Hall.

Strassman, P. 1985. *Information Payoff*. New York: Free Press.

Synnott, William R. 1987. "Putting a CIO in Charge, "*Financial Technology Forum*, December: 47-48.

Thompson, J.D. 1967. *Organizations in Action*. New York: McGraw-Hill.

Toffler, Alvin 1980. *The Third Wave*. New York: William Morrow.

Turner, J. 1985. "Organizational Performance, Size, and the Use of Data Processing Resources," Working Paper # 58, Center for Research in Information Systems, New York University, New York.

Vancil, R. 1983. "Management Systems: Structure and Process." Harvard Business School Working Paper no. 0-183-182.

Vincent, D. R. 1989. "Information Technology--Should You Curtail

Your Investment?" *Financial Executive*, May-June: 51-55.

Von Simson, E. M. 1990. "The Centrally Decentralized IS Organization," *Harvard Business Review*, July-Aug.: 158-62.

Walking, R., & Long, M. 1984. "Agency Theory, Managerial Welfare, and Takeover Bid Resistance," *The Rand Journal of Economics*, 15: 54-68.

Weill, P. 1987. "Information Technology Investment in Utilities," Working Paper #138, Center for Research in Information Systems, New York University, New York.

_____. 1988. *The Relationship Between Investment in Information Technology and Firm Performance in the Manufacturing Sector.* Unpublished Ph.D. dissertation, New York University, New York.

Weill, P. & Olson, M.H. 1989. "Managing Investment in Information Technology: Mini Case Examples and Implications," *MIS Quarterly*, March: 3-16.

Weiner, M., & Girven, J. 1985. "Chief Information Officer: Does Your Company Need One?" *Computerworld*, May 13: ID/2, 4-7.

Whisler, T. L. 1970. *The Impact of Computers on Organizations*. New York: Praeger Publishers.

White, R. 1985. "Agency as Control." In J. Pratt & R. Zeckhauser (eds.), *Principals, and Agents: The Structure of Business*. pp. 187-214. Boston: Harvard Business School Press.

Williams, J. H. 1934. *The Flexible Budget*. New York: McGraw Hill.

Williamson, O.E. 1964. *The Economic Discretionary Behavior: Managerial Objectives in a Theory of the Firm*. Englewood Cliffs, NJ: Prentice Hall.

Wolfson, M. 1985. "Empirical Evidence of Incentive Problems and Their Mitigation in Oil and Gaz Shelter Programs." In J. Pratt & R. Zeckhauser (eds.), *Principals, and Agents: The Structure of Business*, pp. 101-26. Boston: Harvard Business School Press.

Woodward, J. 1970. *Industrial Organization: Behaviour and Control*. London: Oxford University Press.

Zahra, Shaker A., & John A. Pearce II, 1989. "Boards of Directors and Corporate Financial Performance: A Review and Integrative Model," *Journal of Management*, 15(2): 291-334.

Zammuto, R. F. 1982. *Assessing Organizational Effectiveness: Systems Change, Adaptation and Strategy*. Albany, NY: State University Press.

Index

ABOUT THE AUTHOR

ZEINAB A. KARAKE is an Associate Professor of Management at the Catholic University of America in Washington, D.C. She is the author of *Technology and Developing Economies* (Praeger, 1990).